SAN FRANCISCO
C H I L D H O O D

SAN FRANCISCO
C H I L D H O O D

Memories of a great city seen through the eyes of its children

Edited and with an
Introduction by

John van der Zee

GRIZZLY PEAK PRESS
Kensington, California

For information contact:

GRIZZLY PEAK PRESS

350 Berkeley Park Boulevard
Kensington, California 94707
grizzlypeakpress.com

San Francisco Childhood is published by Daniel N. David
and is distributed by Grizzly Peak Press.

Front cover photo courtesy of Ernest Lageson

Design, layout and typesetting by
Liquid Pictures
www.liquidpictures.com

ISBN Number: 978-0-9839264-0-5
Library of Congress Number: 2011936291

Printed in the United States of America

Table Of Contents

❧ *Introduction*

It's a strange place, this small town world city; in the United States, but somehow not really of it: sea-settled, persistently international, a vector for outside influences, fascinating and threatening, mirroring in some ways the relationship of Hong Kong to mainland China. Strange right down to the climate where you can go from Mediterranean blue-and-white to gray Nordic gloom in a modest walk or a dozen bus stops. Where people wear parkas to baseball games and tank tops at a football stadium. Where you can stroll a neighborhood past a block of painted-lady Victorians, round a corner and find yourself amid public housing with kids in hooded sweatshirts idle in mid-day. A city that for all its compact size contains multitudes.

It is among people who were born and/or raised here that this small town world city sense is the strongest. The block you lived on, the playground and school you went to, are still here even if transformed or gentrified. Yet the neighborhood was not some sprawling enclave where you saw, spoke to or did business only with people of your own kind. The fullness of the city in a small space prepares San Franciscans for life in other, often distant places—the multiculturalism, a certain fluency in adapting, knowing how to treat people of different language or dress, where to expect a park, a restaurant, how the buses and subways work—it's all like home in some ways. Plus the people who go away come back: on tour, as visitors, for graduate work, or just to refresh their imaginations. It's a familiar life to step back into, without being accused of forgetting where you came from or putting on airs. Here you can inhabit both large and small worlds and still remain yourself.

San Francisco is an ideal subject for childhood views, because it has never grown up itself. It never had a chance to: Gertrude Atherton, describing the earthquake of 1868, reflects that the city had already burned five times. It was barely twenty years old. With repeated demolition has come constant re-invention: the Gold Rush town became the Silver Kings' town, then the railroad barons' town, the Pacific empire builders', the bankers', the unions', the Navy's, the real-estate developers', the beats', the hippies', the dot-commers', the gays', and now, Asians' and Asian-Americans'. In San Francisco today everyone who makes the city run is Asian: cops, firefighters, bus drivers, cabbies, postal persons, nurses, the CAO, the mayor, *me*—I live as part of three family generations under the same roof, the way Chinese families traditionally do. What is being claimed is what ancestral sweat helped build—gold fortunes, silver fortunes, railroad fortunes. Planting the flag on Gold Mountain.

Fitting, then, that the United Nations was founded here. That its headquarters was supposed to stand on the spot in the Presidio now occupied by Lucasfilm's Industrial Light and Magic. Political re-invention replaced by digital. Who's to say which influence will be broader, more enduring?

It is these two qualities---the complex, world-reflecting character of the city confined in such a limited space, and the changing, never-settled nature of its thematic life—that have determined the contents of this book, so that it seems to represent the city more than the individual writers associated with it. Like the city, it's full of surprises. In choosing the work I did, I have in the process of my own surprise, tried to be inclusive, taking the larger view of childhood to include writers like Maya Angelou, who arrived in San Francisco at 13, only to find herself transformed down to the choice of her name by her experience here. Or Anne Lamott, who was born here, but is mostly associated with Marin County: her key early relationship, with her mother, originated here. At the other end of the scale, I have had to leave out Jack London who, though San Francisco-born owes his childhood to Oakland, and William Saroyan whose signature work took place in San Francisco, but whose birth and boyhood belong to Fresno and, to some degree, the Oakland orphans' home. These are judgment calls and judgment calls are always subject to dispute, but keep in mind that the same judgment that picked these writers also recalled TAD Dorgan, and the Robert Frost of Woodward's Gardens.

Strange too are the congruencies arising from this place: Robert Frost and Jack London, born here within two years of each other, one the son of an unreconstructed Confederate sympathizer, the other of a mother who attempted suicide while pregnant with him; Tad Dorgan and Wilson Mizner, two of the fountainheads of American slang, both beginning their burblings here; Dorgan being succeeded as a cartoonist at the *Bulletin* by another great native cartoonist, Rube Goldberg; Anita Loos applying her own Barbary Coast memories to the screenplay for *San Francisco*; also writing *Gentlemen Prefer Blondes*, the story that was to make her fellow SF-native Carol Channing a star; Robert McNamara, whose earliest local memory was the end of a war, with his reputation made, then ruined, by another war, disputed nowhere more heatedly than here. Why so many curious convergings? Why here? Is it coincidence? Or culture? Perhaps the contents of these stories will help us if not decide then at least understand the city and maybe even ourselves.

I am indebted to Don Ellis of Grizzly Peak Press for suggesting the idea for this book, which is a successor to a similar book, *California Childhood*, that Don published for *Creative Arts Book Co.*, in Berkeley in 1988. To the staff of the San Francisco History Center at San Francisco's Main Public Library. And to my two mentors, Ella and Ronan Kennedy, who have allowed me to see the city I knew as a child through the eyes of its newest generation. I stand, if not on the shoulders of giants, then at least on the sensibilities of some very thoughtful, stimulating and generous individuals.

John van der Zee

SAN FRANCISCO
CHILDHOOD

❧ *Ansel Adams*

Awakening a view of nature that was to enthrall millions

Despite a wiry frame and considerable stamina, as a child I was prone to frequent illness, with far too many colds and flu. I also had extremely poor teeth that plagued me later with diabolic toothaches, especially on cold mountain nights. I now realize that my diet as a child was atrocious: too many sweets and starches and not enough foods with the protein, mineral, and vitamin content I needed. I do not blame my parents for this; there was little knowledge of proper diet in the early 1900s.

My mental state was also precarious. At the age of ten I remember experiencing unsettled periods of weepiness. The doctor ordered me to bed in a darkened room every afternoon for two hours to calm me, but the effect was just the opposite. I remained alert, resistant and hostile to this routine. The sound of the surf from Baker Beach, of the gardener working outside my window, and of occasional children playing near the house created a yearning tension to get up and go that left me in much worse condition. I wanted to run down to the beach in sun, rain, or fog and expend the pent-up physical energy that simply fermented within me. Today I would be labeled hyperactive.

With a resolute whisper, Lobos Creek flowed past our home on its mile-long journey to the ocean. It was bordered, at times covered, with watercress and alive with minnows, tadpoles, and a variety of larvae. Water bugs skimmed the open surfaces and dragonflies darted above the stream bed. In spring, flowers were rampant and fragrant. In heavy fog the creek was eerie, rippling out of nowhere and vanishing into nothingness. I explored every foot, tunneling through the thick brush and following the last small canyons in the clay strata before it met the Pacific. The ocean was too cold for swimming, so I would skirt the wave-foamed edge and follow the rocky shore to Fort Scott to the east or climb along the rugged cliffs to China Beach to the west. These cliffs were dangerous, but I was light and strong and could pull myself by my fingertips over minor chasms.

A beautiful stand of live oaks arched over the creek. In about 1910, the Army Corps of Engineers, for unimaginable reasons, decided to clear out the oaks and brush. My father was out of town when the crime was committed. One of his favorite walks was through these glades to Mountain Lake in the nearby San Francisco Presidio; on his return, he became physically ill when he witnessed the ruthless damage.

I must have been a juvenile problem of consequence, but I was limited by my very proper human surroundings. While my father was liberal in his politics, he was also shy and socially conventional. In the presence of all but close friends he addressed my mother as Mrs. Adams. I never saw him without a collar except on Sunday mornings. Attaching the collar to the shirt by front and back buttons was a major effort. He sometimes yanked the collar off the shirt while making a few pointed remarks about the fate of mankind that such gestures of convention should be so nasty. All his shirts were designed for stiff collars; collarless, he looked quite forlorn, showing a brass button and a long neck.

Certain matters of life were completely avoided or most daringly spoken of in whispers. That did not stop me from asking, "Does God go to the toilet?" Grandfather Bray would clearly enunciate, sometimes between clenched teeth, "Plague be gone, young 'un!"

Inevitably, I pondered the beginnings, wherefrom and how had I entered life? I asked these questions of my mother; she merely shook her head. I enjoyed a prepuberty erection in the bathtub and asked, "What is that?" Again my mother shook her head. I had heard or read mysterious words and would innocently ask neighbors questions such as "What does masturbate mean?" I never had an explanation, only queer looks and obvious evasions. One of the main city sewers drained about a thousand feet or so offshore at Baker Beach, and an array of objects would come ashore. Sanitation was a foreign word in those days and one had to walk carefully on Baker Beach! There also were interesting rubber objects that I first thought were jellyfish, or some other form of sea life. Bringing one home for questioning did not sit well with my mother, and I am confident now that Aunt Mary could not identify it.

I posed my questions to my father and he painfully explained— after being sure we were alone and out of the house. I later learned that he did not have an accurate idea of the essential organs and their relationship. My friends and I, equally uninformed, conjectured the possibilities: never were there greater fantasies in all the paradises of fact or legend!

My favorite hobby was collecting insects. Various bugs filled the bottom drawer of the large bureau with phalanx after phalanx of tiny corpses displayed on pins. When my great-aunt, Mrs. Aurelia Hills Collamore, came from Thomaston, Maine to visit us, she was given my room. She must have been eighty-five years old and was dressed like a Grant Wood woman on Sundays. I told her the bottom drawer of the bureau was full of bugs. Being slightly deaf she misunderstood me, thinking I had said, "Bed bugs!"

There was a screech and a period of feminine demonstration. Even after my explanation, her visit was clouded with the faint possibility that the insects would crawl down from the pins and attack her. I had one huge African black beetle nearly three inches long with a horn like a rhinoceros. It always looked ready for takeoff, and she asked me to please put it somewhere else. I covered it with a little box and put a weight on it. That seemed to mollify her.

To continue my catalog of childhood leisure time activities: I was quite a roller skater for a time until a number of hard falls and close calls with automobiles and horses convinced me I should stop that activity. Another sport I enjoyed for a while was golf. Once, at the old Lincoln Park Golf Links, I lofted a ball over a bunker in the general direction of the hidden green. My companion and I searched for the ball for half an hour (we had a very limited budget for golf balls) and then found it in the cup, an unanticipated hole in one! I played cribbage with my father and pinochle with my friend Billy Prince, and usually lost to both. I tried playing chess, without success, and bridge and poker were anathema. I just could not rouse the patience required to accomplish these games. I also had no interest in spectator sports.

When roaming our neighborhood and the city, I found there was only one rewarding way to get from place to place, and that was to run! I was impatient at the tempo of walking and the slow sidewalk flow of pedestrians and I simply ran, doubtless an object of curiosity. Jogging was unheard of in those days, but a few athletes in training might be seen running in their white shoes, shorts and sweaters. Darting about as I did in a conventional child's suit was out of order and conspicuous. In the late afternoons I usually returned to Baker Beach to walk along the surf-edge across the dark, flame-like tongues of sand. I was never able to find the source of the considerable amount of iron particles that caused this interesting effect. I would take cans of the sand home, dry it out and experiment, sprinkling the sand on a piece of paper and moving magnets of different shapes underneath, producing wonderful patterns with the black iron particles against the white background.

Driftwood would come ashore in all shapes and sizes-
large timbers, poles, wood fragments, and deeply worn parts of
furniture. Some were very beautiful in their configurations. All had
firewood potential. I carried as much as I could home each day to
add to our supply.

The great sand dunes began stirring with developments.
Contractors spawned houses on twenty-five-foot lots. Just east of
our house, two blocks of sand and scrub were graded by scrapers
powered by mules and sweating, yelling men. Baronial limestone
gates were set up at 22nd and 24th Avenues. 23rd Avenue was cut
off and a new street, paralleling Lake Street, was graded in, paved,
with a strip of lawn and a sidewalk on each side and given the
glamorous name of West Clay Street. The basic Clay Street ended
more than a mile away to the East. The imagination is boggled by
the lack of it at times.

Mr. S.A. Born was one of the more dependable and prosperous
contractors and the one who developed the lands surrounding our
home. His houses were contractor designed, put together without
compromise, and have lasted, with a stern dowager quality for
many decades. He was very kind to me, allowing me to visit
his field office and observe his draftsmen. His patience passeth
understanding. From him I learned how to draw a straight line and a
ninety-degree angle. I drew up some plans for houses, forgetting to
provide for stairs and closets.

Words fail to convey my total experience in that office: the
smell of pinewood, ink, and sweat; the all-pervading sand on tables,
chairs, paper, and between teeth; the hot afternoon light coming
through small, dusty, spider-hazed windows, and the sound of wind
and surf invading the room every time the door was opened. There
were rolls and rolls of plans, pale blue and frayed at the edges,
stacked on frames and on the floor, bearing incomprehensible
hieroglyphics of plumbing, wiring, and framing details. The master
carpenter would come in, loudly arguing with gusty profanity some
point, then exit in slam-the-door wrath only to reappear, sanguine,
an hour later.

One day Mr. Born drove me into town and back in his two-cylinder Reo automobile. Proceeding home out Lake Street at eighteen mph with my hands white-knuckled, grasping the jiggling steering wheel, and the engine coughing and clattering under the seat, he yelled, "If a front wheel should come off, we would be crushed to jelly!"

Most of his houses were completed at close to the same time, and they were quickly sold and inhabited. We became an instant neighborhood, a part of San Francisco, no longer loners on the sandy outskirts. Most thought it progress; I wistfully remembered the sand, sea grass, and lupines.

My parents enrolled me in a succession of schools.. From that early period when I was battling institutional education, I too well remember the Rochambeau School. The architect of the school must have been a dull and primitive cubist. It was a dismal three-story building, dark brown on the outside, dark brown and tan on the inside; everything, including its atmosphere, grimly brown. The students acquired this pervading mood of depression from the teachers, and the teachers must have caught it from the building: big square rooms, wide, noisy staircases, grimy windows, ink-stained desks, smudged blackboards, and crummy toilets. The janitor dour, the principal grim, and the playground dirty! Dogs would do and dump on the cement yard; evidences of trysts were occasionally found behind ash cans, the older boys-about-town would grin and wink knowingly.

The school bully, Beasley by name, picked on all the younger and more timid children. He always triumphed without doing too much physical damage. One day he encountered me in an isolated area of the schoolyard. He deftly punched me in the stomach, hard enough to make me gasp. I recall being completely furious. I knew nothing about boxing, but in my blind wrath I swung my fist like a pendulum and swatted him as hard as I could on the chin. To my amazement he toppled over and passed out cold. This was the first time I was personally taken home by the principal.

"Fighting is absolutely not permitted in my school!" the principal exclaimed to my mother.

"Beasley hit me first!" was my excuse.

The principal must have known about Beasley, but she kept silent, glared at me and left.

My mother asked, "Did he hurt you?"   "A little, I guess." Case closed.

By the time I was twelve I had developed a behavior pattern that if I became bored with anything I would drop it; hence my life was cluttered with incomplete expressions. One of my Rochambeau teachers was a Miss Oliver. She was a buxom Minerva with a steady, penetrating stare. Her voice oozed with unctuous certainty as she tried to bring order out of my chaos. Several times she asked me to come to her house for generalized lectures on behavior and responsibility. I did not comprehend most of what she was saying. We would sit in a stuffy little room in which a number of tired plants and an exhausted cat held forth. I remember that I could hear the ocean and yearned to escape the concerned stare and the flow of Truth that cascaded from her pursed lips. I am now sure that she was weaned on misunderstood Emerson.

Each day was a severe test for me, sitting in a dreadful classroom while the sun and fog played outside. Most of the information received meant absolutely nothing to me. For example, I was chastised for not being able to remember what states border Nebraska and what are the states of the Gulf Coast. It was simply a matter of memorizing the names, nothing about the process of memorizing or any reason to memorize. Education without either meaning or excitement is impossible. I longed for the outdoors, leaving only a small part of my conscious self to pay attention to schoolwork.

One day as I sat fidgeting in class the whole situation suddenly appeared very ridiculous to me. I burst into raucous peals of uncontrolled laughter; I could not stop. The class was first amused, and then scared. I stood up, pointed at the teacher, and shrieked my scorn, hardly taking breath in between my howling paroxysms. To the dismay of my mother I was escorted home and remained under house arrest for a week until my patient father concluded that my entry into yet another school would be useless. Instead, I was to study at home under his guidance.

My father was quite good at French and also tutored me through the complexities of basic algebra. He insisted I read the English classics and provided me lessons in ancient Greek with an elderly minister, a Dr. Herriot, who taught me the complexities of that language and its aural magnificence.

Our conversations after the lesson would inevitably lead toward some matter of faith; Dr. Herriot assumed I went to church and he was very curious as to which one. It did no good to explain that I was an agnostic, to him a heathen. My disregard of conventional faith was incomprehensible to him.

One day Dr. Herriot asked what I was currently reading. I told him I was immersed in Shelley's *Prometheus*. He was shocked, and said, "Shelley was a dastardly atheist." I could not understand Dr. Herriot any more than he could me.

Another conversation turned to evolution. "There is no such thing as evolution!" exclaimed Dr. Herriot. "There is only devolution from the year of the Creation!"

I appeared perplexed. He followed with, "We know God created the world in October, four thousand and four years before Christ; we are waiting for the Second Coming which will take place soon! Don't believe this evolution rubbish!"

Now I was stunned. I ventured, "Dr. Herriot, how do you explain the fossils in the rocks?"

The silver-maned Reverend Doctor looked at me with what would pass as theatrical compassion and said, "My dear boy, God put them there to tempt our faith."

After that revelation I could not return to him for further instruction. His cold blue eyes in the ruddy, white-whiskered face, his pronouncement of rigid faith, and his implications of what would happen to me on Judgment Day, all were at huge variance with the luminance of music, the revelations of philosophy and poetry, the freedom of the rolling hills and the ocean.

From my conversations with Dr. Herriot and others came my realization that intolerance, unreason , and exclusionism exist and that all three are blended in many manifestations of our society. This stimulated my intellectual and imaginative faculties, but also drew sharp lines of separation between myself and a good part of the society in which I lived. I believe religion to be deeply personal; I am a loner with my particular amorphous sense of deity.

Sometime in 1914, my father heard me trying to pick out notes on our old upright piano. He decided that his twelve-year-old son had talent! I soon began piano lessons, which were in addition to my other studies.

In 1915 my father gave me a year's pass to the Panama-Pacific International Exposition (celebrating the opening of the Panama Canal), which would be my school for that year. He insisted that I continue my piano and study literature and language at home, but I was to spend a good part of each day at the fair.

The exposition was large, complex, and astounding; a confusion of multitudes of people, more than I had ever encountered, with conversations at excitement levels and innumerable things to see. I visited every exhibit many times during that year.

In some respects it was a tawdry place, a glorious and obviously temporary stage set, a symbolic fantasy, and a dream world of color and style. The buildings, constructed expressly for the exposition, were huge and flamboyant, with great scale and spaciousness. They were to reflect the spirit of classicism, daringly transcribed by western architects and designers. Included were: the Campaniles, reminding me of Italian postcards; the Court of Ages with its infinity of finials, the rococo Hall of Horticulture, the glorious Palace of Fine Arts, and the improbable Tower of Jewels. There were acres of foreign pavilions as well as many from American states, some pleasing and instructive, some incredibly dull.

And then there was the Zone, the amusement area. In addition to the usual neck-breaking rides, tumblers, twisters, and tunnels of love, there were the seamy traps of girlie shows, curio shops, and freak displays. If the fronts of these establishments were bad, the back were worse—plywood, tar paper, trash, as well as drunks and assorted strange fragment of humanity.

On occasion when I was late coming home, I would make for the exits through the backyards of the Zone to the nearest streetcars. On one such evening my path crossed a group of shabby men. One, with a hooked nose and sardonic grin, had rolled up his sleeve and was injecting himself with a huge syringe. I was badly frightened and I rushed through the nearest turnstile and jumped on the first streetcar I saw. It happened to be going in the wrong direction, but no matter. I felt I had escaped some awful, threatening situation. I got home quite late and very distressed. My father asked me what had happened. I blurted out the horror of the experience, but my father simply said, "He must have been a drug addict—you should feel very sorry for him." This clarifying charity eased my spirits.

I happily returned to my school, the exposition. The Festival Hall, a huge, domed building with excellent acoustics, contained an organ, a gargantuan instrument of some quality that now graces San Francisco's Civic Center. Daily at noon the exposition organist, Edwin Lamar, gave a concert that he closed with an improvisation on a theme submitted by someone in the audience. I was increasingly involved in my own music study and was impressed by his ability to create a prelude or a fugue on the spot with such inventiveness, musicianship, and authority. I always tried to attend his concerts, then scampered a mile to the YMCA cafeteria for a cheap lunch.

I made many visits to the painting and sculpture exhibits at the Palace of Fine Arts, where I saw work in the modern vein—Bonnard, Cezanne, Gauguin, Monet, Pissarro, Van Gogh. They had little effect on me at the time, though I remember viewing them repeatedly. I now wonder what subconscious effect they had in the years to follow.

My father often met me in the early afternoon and we visited exhibits together. He particularly enjoyed the science and machinery exhibits and also liked to sit in the courts and watch the fountains. Occasionally my mother and aunt would join us. We would have something to eat and stay for the fireworks; they were always spectacular. Arriving home late, the next day was usually a bit quiet for the ladies.

Although everyone at the exposition was kindly to me, I am sure I was a real pest. But patience is the keystone of salesmanship, and the intent of the exposition was to encourage interest in and purchase of the items displayed. It was much more sensible than ordinary advertising; everything was there to see and handle and try out if you wished. Exhibitors seemed interested in inquisitive children and went out of their way to explain things. They were anxious that word be spread at home and parents alerted to such things as new office or home equipment.

A friend of my father was managing the Dalton Adding Machine Company exhibit and he taught me how to use the machine. I enjoyed demonstrating it to spectators and often did so for an hour or two a day.

I also frequented the Underwood Typewriter exhibit that presented on a large movable stage dioramas of the history of office writing—from the eighteenth-century bookkeeper laboriously pushing a quill pen to the most modern typewriter of 1915. These scenes appeared in sequence, one dissolving into another with a smoothness that was truly remarkable. Real people were involved; each illusion was a beautifully arranged and illuminated stage set. How it was done baffled everyone

I met Mr. Thomas Mooney, the technician of the display, and he revealed the secret, making me promise not to divulge it until the exposition was over. I was proud of this confidential information and carefully guarded the secret. It is hard to describe my astonishment and disbelief a few days after the shocking 1917 Preparedness. Day bombing on Market Street to see a photograph of Thomas J. Mooney, charged with major complicity in this terrible crime. I found it difficult to believe he was guilty, but he was so charged and sentenced to many years in prison. In my memory he is a kind and gentle man.

On the closing day of the exposition, I arrived early and visited my old haunts. Many displays were already packed up, leaving a sad, abandoned look. I had saved up some cash for a few rides on the roller coaster, and then had a double-rich dinner at the YMCA cafeteria. Piles of turkey and dressing and ice cream went the way of my innards. I had one last ride on the roller coaster with disastrous gastronomic results and ended my activities at the infirmary.

I left the infirmary at nine in the evening and wandered off to the east gate. The crowd was huge, filling the large open areas from rim to rim. I was trapped in the center of a vast surge of people who swayed en masse as if under the spell of a choreographer. It was terrifying; several women fainted but were kept upright by the close-pressing bodies. We slowly reached the exit and poured into the street. The streetcars were jammed; there was little use waiting, so I started to walk home through the Presidio. I found that I was quite weak, the combination of illness and the long, frightening experience in that mindless throng had their effect. I needed to rest frequently and simply sat down on the roadside. I straggled home at two A.M. to find my family anxiously awaiting me, fearing the worst.

After the exposition, my education continued along its individual course. In and out of several schools in search of a legitimizing diploma, I finally ended up at the Wilkins School. Mrs. Kate Wilkins was a stout, motherly character; she read the lessons out loud to me and gave me an A. Graduating from the eighth grade at the Wilkins School signaled the end of my formal academic career.

I often wonder at the strength and courage my father had in taking me out of the traditional school situation and providing me with these extraordinary learning experiences. I am certain he established the positive direction of my life that otherwise, given my native hyperactivity, could have been confused and catastrophic. I trace who I am and the direction of my development to those years of growing up in our house on the dunes, propelled especially by an internal spark tenderly kept alive and glowing by my father.

"Childhood" and author photo from ANSEL ADAMS: AN AUTOBIOGRAPHY by Ansel Adams with Mary Street Alinder, a New York Graphic Society Book, Boston, Little Brown & Co., 1985. Reprinted by permission of the Ansel Adams Publishing Rights Trust.

✎ *Robert Frost*

The great New England poet's San Francisco childhood memories

A PECK OF GOLD

Dust always blowing about the town,
Except when sea fog laid it down,
And I was one of the children told
Some of the blowing dust was gold.

All the dust the wind blew high
Appeared like gold in the sunset sky,
But I was one of the children told
Some of the dust was really gold.

Such was life in the Golden Gate:
Gold dusted all we drank and ate,
And I was one of the children told,
"We all must eat our peck of gold."

AT WOODWARD'S GARDENS

A boy, presuming on his intellect,
Once showed two little monkeys in a cage
A burning glass they could not understand.
Words are no good: to say it was a lens
For gathering solar rays would not have helped.
But let him show them how the weapon worked.
He made the sun a pinpoint on the nose
Of the first one, then the other, till it brought
A look of puzzled dimness to their eyes
That blinking could not seem to blink away.
They stood arms laced together at the bars,
And exchanged troubled glances over life.
One put a thoughtful hand up to his nose
As if reminded—or as if perhaps
Within a million years of an idea.
He got his purple little knuckles stung.
The already known had once more been confirmed
By psychological experiment,
And that were all the finding to announce
Had the boy not presumed too close and long.
There was a sudden flash of arm, a snatch,
And the glass was the monkey's, not the boy's.
Precipitally, they retired back-cage

And instituted an investigation
On their part, though without the needed insight.
They bit the glass, and listened for the flavor.
They broke the handle and the binding off it.
Then none the wiser, frankly gave it up,
And having hid it in their bedding straw
Against the day of prisoners' ennui,
Came dryly forward to the bars again
To answer for themselves:
Who said it mattered
What monkeys did or didn't understand?
They might not understand a burning-glass.
They might not understand the sun itself.
It's knowing what to do with things that counts.

Note: Robert Frost, the emblematic New England poet, was born in San Francisco in 1876. Woodward's Gardens was a combination private park, menagerie, museum and restaurant that operated in the Mission District between 1865 and 1891. It made such an impression on the young Frost that its memory still moved him to poetry half a century later.

✎ *Gertrude Atherton*

Slipping up and down the social scale, occasionally on slipping ground.

I was born on Rincon Hill, a slight elevation south of Market Street and covered with roomy houses in pleasant gardens, two or three of which lingered there until the fire of 1906. Rincon Hill, South Park at its feet, Folsom and two or three other streets near-by, and, in the north, running up the hill, Stockton Street and its immediate western neighbors, were the only places in those days where one could be born respectably.

For a short time the young couple lived with my grandfather, who had taken the house for a year. The dislike between Mr. Uhlhorn [stepfather] and myself was, from the first, mutual and intense. He regarded me, and justly, as a spoilt brat; why I hated him I do not know, but I did, and delighted in annoying him in every way my fertile mind could conceive. The climax came one day when I hurtled down the banisters and almost knocked him over, big as he was.

My mother, anxious for her new-found happiness, packed me off to a small boarding-school on Ellis Street, kept by two Hollanders, Mrs. Wilson and Mrs. Reynolds. And there a singular event happened which I have never been able to interpret. Something valuable disappeared. Questions failing to elicit any information, we were all, boarders, day-scholars, and servants, summoned into the darkened parlor where Mrs. Wilson sat with a basket in her lap. We could barely see a small still black animal in the basket, and no children were ever more frightened. Mrs. Reynolds stood by the door to prevent a precipitate retreat.

"You will all of you," said Mrs. Wilson, in a deep ominous voice, "pass in turn and lay your hand on this creature, and when the guilty one touches it there will be a growl—but it will not hurt you."

Terrified and shaking, we dragged ourselves forward and did as we were told. It was a slimy beast and our palms were black when we withdrew them. There was no result. The enigma did not even whimper.

This singular performance in the darkened parlor was by no means as strange as what followed, for the inference is natural that Mrs. Wilson expected the criminal to be nervous and pinch the thing until it squealed; but the next morning when we who boarded there awoke, we found the palms of our hands black and slimy. I slept in a large room with three other children, a cot in each corner, and was awakened by hysterical screams. One of my companions had awakened first and the mere thought of contact in her sleep with that disgusting object drove her frantic. No explanation was ever vouchsafed us. Nor, as far as I know, was the valuable possession, whatever it may have been, recovered. I have asked several Hollanders if they knew of this singular version of trial by ordeal, and the answer has always been in the negative.

Mr. Uhlhorn left the Quartermaster's Department, entered the brokerage business, and prospered for a while. His family, highly pleased with him at this time, advanced the capital.

As my grandfather, his lease expired, went into lodgings, he took a house on Oak Grove Avenue, a short street running, I think, from Folsom to Brannan, lined with fine residences in gardens and a row of new tall brown houses, in one of which we were handsomely installed. My mother, now reinstated in Society, went out constantly to dinners and parties; she sometimes came into my room to say goodnight before leaving, but I remember only one of her gowns: a bright green corded silk, trimmed with crepe leaves, which inspired me with the ambition to grow up at once and inherit it.

It was the fashion in those days to be plump, and she had a tiny waist between "swelling hips" and a low full bust. Her shoulders were magnificent. She had as many admirers as ever, but eyes for no one but her husband.

I was all ears and overheard much gossip when I was supposed to be reading fairy tales in a corner of the large front bedroom and my mother was enjoying an afternoon visit from her more intimate friends. Of course, the talk was all of dress, personalities, and scandals; what else did they have to talk about? Scandal made no impression on me, but I was very much interested in this and that about the "belles": the "three Macs," Ella Maxwell, Mollie McMullen, and Jennie McNulty; my future sisters-in-law, Alejandra and Elena Atherton. Another, whose tragic story I have told in *A Daughter of the Vine*, was Nelly Gordon, whose father had built South Park. Even then there were rumors that she "drank," and her terrible old mother, never seen, was supposed to be in a perpetual state of inebriety.

I believe Bret Harte, employed in the Mint—was a beau at that time. And an expert at Croquet! But although my grandfather and mother knew him, I never saw him. He made Alejandra Atherton, who was half Spanish, the heroine of several of his stories.

There was a picture of Mark Twain in an album Mr. Uhlhorn had brought from New York, and I dimly remember a tall man with bushy hair and eyebrows coming one night to dinner; I caught but a glimpse of him in the hall below as I hung over the banisters in my nightgown. He was on his way round the world before writing *Innocents Abroad*. It was published by subscription and I can recall the excitement when the large calf-bound book arrived. Everybody discussed it for months, whether they read it or not.

Poor Mr. Uhlhorn was forced to endure me at this time. My mother, indignant at the ordeal to which I had been subjected by "two superstitious fools," sent me to another boarding-school, but I was returned with thanks at the end of the first day. I had demoralized the school by turning somersaults in the classrooms. There was nothing to do but put up with me at home, but as time passed I disliked Mr. Uhlhorn too thoroughly to annoy him. When he noticed me at all, it was with an icy politeness that left me with no recourse but to run my tongue out at him. I kept out of his way.

Why the children in the neighborhood played with me I cannot imagine (unless it were on account of my abundant toys which I gave away freely), for I generally finished the hour by beating them up, and one I threw down-stairs. Nurses were a problem, for none would remain more than a month. This problem, however, was solved when my sister Aleece was born, and the wet-nurse offered to take me over. She had three children of her own and announced grimly that she "guessed she could manage me or know the reason why."

This remarkable woman, Rose Stoddard, forced by a worthless husband to go out and support her children, came to us for a short period and remained in the family for thirty-five years—the most devoted, loyal, all-enduring creature I have ever known. And she knew how to manage me. She spanked me with gusto—no other nurse had been permitted to touch my sacred person—but she won my affection and interest by more subtle methods. She coaxed me to read to her and to learn poetry for her entertainment, and she sang, at the top of her voice, the most rollicking of Irish songs. And I never tired of listening to the stories of her own life, her children, and friends.

She was very fat and I used to sit regarding with fascinated eyes my frail little sister tugging at one of her enormous breasts— which she would exhibit with superb indifference on anyone's front door step, in a shop, or in a street car; with Aleece cradled in her big strong arms—she disdained a baby carriage—she took me for long walks every day, and when we were tired boarded a car and rode all over town. Sometimes we called on her friends in the humbler quarters and they treated me to jam and ginger-bread. These visits were always the reward of excessive virtue on my part, and when deprived of them for a week I wept stormily.

But she by no means exterminated the imp in me and there were times when it broke out. I remember distinctly one evening when my sister was ill and restless and Rose dared not put her down nor even raise her voice. She had a new hat my mother had given her and was looking forward to wearing it on her next visit to less fortunate friends. I took this hat from the wardrobe and, seating myself before her—at a safe distance—snipped it to pieces with a large pair of scissors. I shall never forget the rumbling accompaniment of billingsgate, for she had a broad Irish tongue and could use the most terrible language. I was dealt with later on.

My mother had a singular habit, peculiar perhaps to her time. Every now and then she would draw the curtains of her bedroom, lie down on the sofa, announce that she was going to have the blues, and was not to be disturbed. There she would remain, sometimes for three days, refusing to eat or speak. Everybody would go about on tiptoe. Mr. Uhlhorn retired to the spare bedroom. Then she would suddenly come to, bathe and dress herself, and be as gay and charming as ever. Whether this morbid indulgence was due to the fact that blues were the fashion, or she was tired of everybody and wanted to rest, or because melancholy for some reason really overwhelmed her, or pure cussedness, was a problem I never solved. But upon her revival she was always treated like a queen and every one hastened to obey her lightest behest.

Mr. Uhlhorn must have got a position of some sort through the influence of one of his few remaining friends, for when Aleece was three and Daisy two we moved into a fashionable boarding-house in San Francisco on the corner of Market and Powell Streets. Here the endless pageant from the window amused me (I remember the first parade of the laborers for an eight-hour day), and as I was now twelve and somewhat improved in behavior I was allowed, Rose having her hands full with the two children, to go to school alone and roam about the neighborhood. I made friends with a number of booksellers and perched on their counters for hours at a time. They were amused at my precocity and lent me books. One even let me "tend shop." Occasionally my father sent his old darky servant for me on Sundays and took me to my Uncle Ben's mansion on Rincon Hill or to his country house on Lake Merritt in Oakland. My father at this time had lost his money, and received no help from his brother who was as stingy as he was rich. Not long after, however, he went down and my father went up, and supported him until his apoplectic death.

But that time is forever made memorable by the great earthquake of 1868. It was eight o'clock in the morning and I was in my mother's large corner bedroom. Rose had gone down-stairs to get the children's breakfast. My mother and I were awaiting her return before going to the dining room. Mr. Uhlhorn must have been away.

Suddenly there was a low menacing roar, then a terrific upheaval that flung the house about like a cork on the waters, accompanied by the horrid sound of protesting masonry, running feet, and piercing screams. My mother stood as if turned into stone. The wardrobe walked out into the middle of the room. An immense crystal chandelier gave a mighty swing. Aleece was standing directly underneath it. Obeying a blind instinct I sprang forward and rushed her to the other side of the room just as it snapped and fell. At this moment Rose burst into the room, her hands full of bread. Muttering "My God! My God! My God! Holy Mary! Holy Mary!" she slung Aleece under one arm and Daisy under the other, still holding on to the bread, and, with the surprising agility of the stout, ran down two flights of stairs and out into the street. I followed her through halls crowded with gasping hysterical women, many of them in scant attire. Only Judge and Mrs. Morrison, standing in their doorway, were entirely composed and laughed heartily at the vision of fat Rose with a kicking child under each arm, her hands maintaining their firm grasp on the bread. I was probably goggle-eyed; I had not been frightened upstairs but flight induced panic. As I passed Mrs. Morrison she said, "What are you afraid of, my child? It is only an earthquake." But I dashed on. I had always found safety with Rose.

The city had already burned down five times, but on this occasion, with greater provocation than ever before, it was miraculously spared. By half-past eight all were seated at breakfast in the dining room volubly relating their "experiences." More than one had been in the bathtub. Nor was there any loss of life in San Francisco, although, had the earthquake occurred half an hour later, it might have taken a heavy toll: a number of buildings were in process of erection and many workmen would have been perched precariously on the scaffoldings.

Shortly after, we moved into a pleasant little house on Jones Street. But there was no superfluous money, no more parties, no more entertaining at home. We lived a very quiet life and only old and tried friends came to the house. Mr. Uhlhorn and my mother quarreled a good deal (I grew up with the idea that the matrimonial condition was a succession of bickerings), but she was still devoted to him, and as he was out a good deal at night no doubt she was jealous of him.

Rose found a good cook, and was chambermaid as well as nurse.

This blessed interval may have lasted for two years. Mr. Uhlhorn had promised my mother to gamble no more and his salary amply covered the household expenses. Rose sang at her work once more.

Then came the debacle.

There was gloom in the house. Even I, who cared for nothing but reading at this time, running home from school to bury my nose in a story-book, knew that something dire had happened. My mother was white and tearful. Mr. Uhlhorn silent and sullen, and always in the house. Rose muttered under her breath.

Then one night, Rose, running across me in the hall, told me sharply not to go near the front bedroom; Mr. Uhlhorn was ill. I accordingly went to the door and looked in. He lay sprawled on the bed, fully dressed, his eyes closed, and breathing stertorously. I did not know until long after that he had tried to kill himself with chloroform. My mother was standing motionless by his side looking down at him.

Terrified, I ran back to my room and shut myself in. But I did not go to bed nor did I read. Tragedy was in the air, and no doubt we were in for a new series of misfortunes; but I think that, even as in my future life when death or any sort of disaster impended, I was chiefly moved by a sense of drama. Mingled with apprehension was a keen expectation of something interesting to come.

It came at midnight. Prowling about the house, but keeping out of the way of Rose, I heard a carriage drive up to the door. I ran to the head of the stairs and hung over the banisters, marveling to hear my grandfather's voice as Rose opened the front door.

He was a slow-moving man as a rule, but tonight he ascended the stairs rapidly. His face, usually benignant, was white and set, his eyes almost glaring behind the gold-rimmed spectacles that always seemed a part of him. I ran forward to greet him, but he brushed me aside and strode into the room where Mr. Uhlhorn, in overcoat and hat, his mouth flaccid, his expression vacuous, a bag in his hand, stood swaying on his feet.

My grandfather, without a word, seized him by the arm, dragged him out of the room and down the stairs. In another moment the carriage drove off. I learned in due course that my grandfather put Mr. Uhlhorn on board a ship bound for South America, and told him never to show his face in California again. He had forged the name of his employer for a large amount—probably to pay his gambling debts—and the victim forbore to prosecute out of friendship for my grandfather and on condition that he left the country at once.

But no influence could keep it out of the newspapers, and public humiliation was added to my mother's despairing grief. She was completely crushed. For days she did not speak, and doubtless she would have fallen into a state of melancholia had not Daisy come down with varioloid. There was a smallpox epidemic in the city.

Smallpox epidemics were no novelty in San Francisco at that period of its history, nor for many years after. I was never without a camphor bag round my neck, and when going to and from school, made wide detours to avoid houses displaying the warning yellow flag. The pest house, out in the sand wastes, became so crowded during these epidemics that additional victims were isolated in their own houses. It was sometime during the eighties that Dr. Mears became Health Officer and made a house-to-house campaign, vaccinating everyone in the city. There has never been a smallpox epidemic since.

My mother was forced out of her semi-coma and nursed my sister, whose life for a time was despaired of. Aleece and I had chicken pox, and between the three of us she had little time to think, and her mental health was restored.

❧ *Mae Ngai*

From Chinese to Chinese-American.

The Chinese girl was the only nonwhite child at the home. Her Chinese name was never recorded in America, and she herself never acknowledged it. She was called Mary McGladery, after the assistant matron who took her in, just a few months after she arrived in San Francisco in 1868, at the age of eleven. She came from somewhere near Shanghai, unaccompanied by any adult relation. It was later said that she was an orphan brought by Christian missionaries, but there is no evidence to confirm this. If missionaries brought her, it is unclear what led them to abandon her once they arrived.

Many years later, after her death, her son would say that she came from an "aristocratic Pekin family." If that claim was true, the whole truth would be even more tragic. The girl's mother would likely have been a number-two or number-three wife, a concubine,

discarded for displeasing her master—perhaps for not bearing a
son—and destitute, forced to sell or give away her daughter. The
girl may have been traded again before ultimately ending up in
California, brought as an indentured servant, what the Cantonese
called a *mui tsai.*

Mui tsai were common in China. They were daughters of
impoverished parents, sold into domestic servitude until the age of
eighteen, at which time they were to be released into marriage. A
mui tsai was bound to her mistress, received no wages, and had no
legal recourse in the event of abuse. Formally considered a form
of charity for poor girls, the mui tsai system did treat some girls
well. But others bore heavy workloads, beatings, and rape. The
most unfortunate were not freed upon majority but were instead
resold into prostitution.

The mui tsai brought to California in the nineteenth century
were sometimes servants in Chinese merchants' families, but more
often they were connected to the prostitution industry. They were
brought to perform menial and domestic work in the brothels of
Chinatown and were generally intended for prostitution when
they became older. Sex trafficking was, as always, lucrative for
the traffickers. Brothel owners earned $2,500 a year on each
prostitute, far more than the $500 average annual income for a
Chinese immigrant.

From the 1850s through 1875, several thousand Chinese
women immigrated to California. By 1860, eight years before
Mary's arrival, there were 654 Chinese women living in San
Francisco, not a small number, though still dwarfed by the male
population, which accounted for 95 percent of the Chinese in
America. Euro-American travel writers, journalists, police,
missionaries, and census takers believed that save for a handful of
merchants' wives with bound feet, nearly all Chinese women in the
city were prostitutes—according to the census, as many as 97 percent
in 1860 and 72 percent in 1870. A Euro-American writer described
Chinese women arriving in port in 1872 as being "from the lowest
class, and often of the vilest character."

Prostitutes of all kinds were numerous in the West, both in towns and in the mining areas, where there were relatively few women. Contrary to popular perception, most prostitutes in mid-nineteenth-century San Francisco were white women. Those who came from the East to work in western brothels ranged from independent spirits to fallen women. Among the Chinese, there were a handful of high-class courtesans who entertained white men , such as the famous Atoy, who was said to be so beautiful that it cost an ounce of gold (worth sixteen dollars) just to look at her. But most Chinese prostitutes were trapped in debased conditions. Americans called both mui tsai and Chinese prostitutes "slave girls."

Not all Chinese women in San Francisco were sex workers, however. Some worked as shoe binders, servants, tailors, launderers, and gardeners. They were wives of merchants, fishermen, and workingmen. Some of the single women in Chinatown may have been living in the manner of the *zishu nu* (self-combed women) of the Pearl River delta, independent "sworn sisters" who lived in "girls' houses" and worked in the textile workshops. Yet the association of Chinese women with prostitution was widespread, a perception paralleling the notion that Chinese men were "coolies." The growing sense that Chinese were a racial menace to white society was fueled in part by the stereotypes of Chinese coolies and prostitutes.

By the time of the girl's journey to America in 1868, steamships had been introduced in transpacific travel. She would have come on one of the four wooden-hulled side-wheelers put into service the year before by the Pacific Mail Steamship Company, when it won the U.S. government contract to carry mail between San Francisco and Yokohama and Hong Kong. The Pacific Mail's wharf now had two arched entries—marked "PMSS-Co. New York and Panama" and "PMSS-Co. China via Japan"—both to the "East." The transpacific mail service inaugurated the first regularly scheduled crossings between the United States and East Asia and obviously carried much more than mail.

Contemporaries noted that the steamers were "richly furnished and luxuriously fitted," with "splendid smoking saloon[s]" on the main deck. These novelties were aimed at attracting European and American passengers, but the real business remained in cargo and third-class accommodation, or steerage. The Pacific Mail both anticipated and generated a high volume of trade and emigration from China. A writer observing the arrival of the *America* in November 1869 wrote, "She is the largest vessel I have ever seen… Built with all the modern improvements in naval architecture, and also with a view to the greatest practical usefulness, she is capable of bearing a large number of classes of passengers. The travel of white persons between here and China is comparatively small, but that of Chinese greater."

If the girl had been brought to San Francisco by missionaries, she would have traveled with them in cabin class, which was expensive—upwards of $200 a ticket—although missionaries enjoyed discounted rates. But if she'd been shipped as a mui tsai to work in a brothel, she would have traveled in steerage. Although steam travel improved accommodations for cabin-class passengers on the Pacific routes, steerage conditions remained poor, well below so-called European steerage, the standard set by the transatlantic immigration trade. The area below decks was divided into large, dimly lit compartments, each arranged with two or even three narrow berths one above the other. Each compartment accommodated as many as two hundred people, along with their baggage. "Women's steerage" separated the sexes. Ventilation and light were scant; privacy was nonexistent. Because steerage was located forward and amidships, close to the engine room and the enormous paddle wheels, noise and vibrations were constant. Yet conditions in Asiatic steerage were not as bad as those aboard the coolie ships bound for South America, which carried indentured workers to plantations as replacements for African slaves. Even at age eleven, the girl may have understood that ship conditions for Chinese travelers were a reflection of their place in the colonial world order, with coolies a notch above enslaved Africans and voluntary emigrants a notch below Europeans.

It is possible that the girl arrived on the *Colorado*, which steamed into San Francisco on August 16, 1868. The ship carried twenty thousand packets of tea and silk, along with eighty passengers in cabin class and eight hundred Chinese in steerage. The girl might have been one of the unnamed members of two parties traveling in cabin class: Reverend A. Folsom with his wife, two children, and servant; and Choy Chew with his "w'fe & s'vt." But more likely she was one of thirty women and girls traveling in steerage. The *Colorado* had left Hong Kong in June, stopping in Yokohama and at the coaling station on Brooks Island (later renamed Midway), the first extra-continental territory claimed by the United States, in 1859, as a commercial and naval outpost. The voyage was unusually long and rough—sixty-eight days in strong headwinds.

Upon arrival in San Francisco, the girl was likely met at the dock by someone from the brothel. The procurers or their representatives routinely met the women and girls who came under contract to them, took them directly to the Chinese quarter, and put them to work. The labor of a brothel mui tsai was similar to that of a domestic servant—cleaning floors, emptying slop buckets, and doing other household chores—but in addition to her arduous labor, a mui tsai had to endure involuntary confinement in a house of prostitution.

Instead of going directly to a brothel, the girl may have been detained by the police when she stepped off the boat. During the 1860s, huiguan [native place or surname association] leaders attempted to thwart the "traffickers in frail humanity" by asking the police to detain all female passengers on arriving ships. Huiguan representatives would then question the women and deliver bona fide wives to their husbands, while holding the rest for return to China on the next outbound steamer. The strategy worked for a while, but by the late 1860s, brothel owners were getting their women released by petitioning the court on the women's behalf for habeas corpus. The judges tended to discharge the women (none admitted to being brought to the United States for prostitution), although they would not release young girls. In one case, the court placed two teenage girls in the care of the Magdalen Asylum, an Irish-Catholic home for former prostitutes. In another, two "very young girls" were remanded to the sheriff's custody.

Whether she ran away from her procurers or was placed in the care of the sheriff, a few months after her arrival the girl came to the attention of Reverend Augustus Loomis, head of the Presbyterian Chinese mission in Chinatown. She may have escaped from her keepers, perhaps while sent out on an errand, with a kind soul taking her to the "Jesus man," or she may have been referred by the sheriff. She then became the charge of Reverend Loomis. But what was he to do with her? His wife had recently died, and Loomis had neither the time nor the facilities to care for a young girl. He may have wanted to place her in the home of a Chinese-Christian family, but that was risky, for no one could have safely harbored a runaway slave girl in Chinatown without fear of reprisal and abduction. The Magdalen Asylum was not appropriate—it was for fallen women, not young girls, and it was a Catholic home besides. So Loomis brought the girl to the Ladies' Society home. Although the home cared only for white children, the matron could not refuse the minister and the frightened girl. This was not an ordinary case, but one that involved a rescue from "slavery."

At the home, the girl joined some eighty other children. Miss McGladery found her particularly bright and took considerable interest in raising her. She taught her not only to read but also to play the piano and to draw. Under Miss McGladery's tutelage, young Mary became a genteel, westernized girl in a Chinese body, her former Chinese self repressed into the unconscious.

The Chinese girl called Mary McGladery was one of the first Chinese "slave girls" to be rescued by the Protestant missionaries in San Francisco. Her story was not publicized, although the missionaries who met her were inspired to commence work among Chinese women and children. Prior to this time, the missionaries had focused their attention on male Chinese laborers, reaching out to them by offering English-language classes and by visiting their places of work. Women were harder to approach because they remained indoors, whether as wives of merchants and workers or as prostitutes. Mary's arrival at the home may have prompted the president of the Ladies' Society and other Protestant women to organized the Women's Union Mission of San Francisco to Chinese Women and Children in 1869. The Women's Union employed Mrs. Sing Mi, a bilingual Christian, to translate for white missionary women during home visits and discussed plans to start a school for Chinese children.

Mary also inspired the Methodist missionary Reverend Otis Gibson to take up work among Chinese women. Gibson paid a visit to the Ladies' Society home in 1869, after Mary had been there for a few months, and saw "one or two Chinese women" who had "escaped their cruel servitude" and been brought to the home by Reverend Loomis. Although Loomis was already advocating for "some home or house of refuge" for the pitiable prostitutes, it was Gibson who created a "female department" at his mission house. His wife organized the Women's Missionary Society of the Pacific Coast in 1870. But the missionaries did not know how to establish contact with prostitutes. It was a year before the first woman came to Gibson's mission home—a woman who had tried to drown herself in the bay and was brought to the mission by the police. More women came as word of the refuge slowly spread.

It would be another decade before rescue became a public project, with sensational raids of brothels and success narratives of rescued prostitutes converted to Christianity, taught English, trained in the domestic arts, and married off to Chinese-Christian men. The first girls and women were rescued quietly and without publicity. Anonymity allowed them to deny their pasts, bury their shame, and become new people. In Mary's case, silence about her experiences before she arrived at the home was a prerogative she would exercise throughout her life.

Mary was eighteen years old when she met Jeu Dip in the spring of 1875; he was twenty-three. If she still spoke Chinese, it was not any of the Cantonese dialects that were prevalent among the immigrants. So Jeu Dip courted the Chinese girl named Mary McGladery in English. In fact, both of them spoke English well, if not fluently, learning it as they had at a young age and through virtual immersion. They were, in other words, fast becoming Chinese Americans.

To be Chinese American in 1875 was to be something new. No one yet used the term to suggest hybridity or assimilation. Nearly all Chinese in San Francisco were first-generation immigrants, and even the merchant families with American-born children lived and worked in the Chinese quarter and were not acculturated to American ways. Jeu Dip and Mary McGladery were different; they had come to America without Chinese parents and lived among Euro-Americans. Their ability to speak English, their manner of dress, and their everyday practice—he in the public sphere of commerce and she in the domestic arts—indicated their acculturation. At the same time, they were the only Chinese in their respective worlds and were thus marked by a double difference—different from the white people around them, different from other Chinese.

When they met, each was poised on the cusp of adulthood, facing a future that was not without possibility but also was uncertain. No one really knew what it meant to be "Chinese American" in a world that separated Chinese from Americans culturally, socially, and spatially. Jeu Dip and Mary McGladery recognized in each other a kindred spirit, another rare and marginal subject. Perhaps she sat next to him atop the milk wagon while he lingered outside the home; maybe they took walks along the dusty streets in the neighborhood. They probably spoke about their dreams—he to have his own business, she perhaps to pursue music or painting. They also no doubt encouraged each other. Despite knowing that Chinese were not favored in California, they perhaps felt justified in their confidence because they knew they were different from other Chinese.

But if Jeu Dip and Mary McGladery were both prototypical Chinese Americans, they had come to their new identities along different psychic routes. We can piece together enough of Mary's background to know that her experience must have been traumatic. By contrast, Jeu Dip appears to have had a kind of cunning, a combination of smarts and good luck that enabled him to turn situations to his favor. His own repression of the past seems to have been more a product of will than of trauma. Like Mary, he was a survivor, but he had never had to put himself entirely into the hands of another or remake himself in that person's image. He was full of confidence and ambition. He was determined to be his own man, and he played each chance he got to the fullest.

❧ *TAD*

By S.J. Perelman

A great humorist on the humorist who inspired him.

Back in the spring of 1947, a fattish young potentate in the
Federated Malay States named the Tunghu Makhota, His Highness
Ismail, Grandfather of the Shrine, Commander of The Most Noble
and Exalted Order of St. Michael and St. George, Prince Regent and
Heir Apparent to the throne of Johore, gave a luncheon party in his
domain for 14 guests. The Prince Regent, his skin glowing with
a fresh coat of Mazola, was clad in a purple sport shirt worn over
pants apparently woven from pliofilm, since from time to time they
afforded an unexciting glimpse of underdrawers. His two wives
wore lace bajus that encased more piquant charms; asparkle on the
bosom of the senior was a diamond of sufficient candlepower to

illuminate a supermarket opening in Los Angeles. Twelve of the guests were British colonial administrators and rubber planters, of the type catalogued by Somerset Maugham, and their lemon-colored ladies, dehydrated, marcelled, and chiffoned to the teeth. The remaining two were a couple of seedy wandervogels rambling around the world on a shoestring—specifically Al Hirschfeld, the caricaturist, and the present writer. Following the repast, a number of the distinguished company felt called upon to eulogize the host, and their tongues loosened by the grape, clacked away like so many metronomes. The most garrulous was a scarlet-faced old blimp, with a nose Hirschfeld likened to an exploded eggplant, who bumbled through a tribute that almost unhinged one's reason. Midway in his discourse, my companion leaned over and apostrophized the speaker in two words. "Judge Rummy," he whispered in my ear.

Lest any law student start combing the annals of the American Bar Association for a clue to the identity of Judge Rummy, he can be spared the trouble. Judge Rumhauser ("Call me Rummy") was one of the cherished cartoon characters of my boyhood—the creation of T.A. Dorgan, the comic artist known as Tad, whose drawings endeared him to millions of newspaper readers in the early decades of this century. The judge and Silk Hat Harry, his crony, adversary and rival in love, were the protagonists of a strip called "Silk Hat Harry's Divorce Suit," the lesser figures of which bore such names as Bunk, Fedinck, Reno Ruth and Frisco Fannie. Curiously enough, the origin of the strip was a classic law case, the trial of Harry K. Thaw for the murder of Stanford White. Tad conceived it as a burlesque and lampooned the proceedings so unmistakably that he was threatened with libel more than once, but it ran for 20 years without interruption. Its theme, if so lofty a word is permissible, was the frailty of marriage; Judge Rummy and Harry were shameless womanizers, constantly on the prowl in court and out, resorting to any stratagem to steal each other's popsies. What made the feature momentous, however, and elevated it to greatness was that all its characters were dogs in human dress; everyone in sight—judge and jury, appellants, lawyers, bailiffs and even the fashionably attired spectators in the courtroom—had ears

like poodles and spaniels. Other than this playful touch, the strip
was totally devoid of sentimentality—quite the reverse, in fact. As
Stephen Becker noted in his *Comic Art in America*, "these were
cynical, egotistical dogs, looking out for No. 1, with no sympathy for
the fool or the weakling." Like all of Tad's characters, they were a
distillation of his random, disenchanted views of life. His history is
worth a brief interpolation.

CHICKEN FANCIERS AT THE MARKET

The proverbial silver spoon was nowhere in evidence when
Thomas Aloysius Dorgan was born in 1877 in a San Francisco
tenement, and least of all when, at the age of 13, an accident crippled
his right hand beyond any further use. He left school at 14, and
despite this infirmity, obtained a job in the art department of the
Bulletin; he drew there, and subsequently at the *Chronicle* and the
Examiner for the next 15 years. By 1902 his work had attracted
such notice that William Randolph Hearst, searching for a political
cartoonist of the stature of Thomas Nast to satirize Tammany Hall,
transferred him to the *New York Evening Journal*. Though his biting
caricatures of Murphy, the Tammany boss, greatly aided Hearst
in his campaign for the New York mayoralty, the publisher was
defeated, and thereafter Tad devoted his talent to sports. His widely
syndicated sketches and reports of championship fights in that era
first made him popular with the sporting fancy, but it was "Silk Hat

Harry's Divorce Suit" and the successive series, "Indoor Sports" and
"Outdoor Sports" that won a huge national audience.

   The two latter were caustic, single panel portraits of the genus
nudnik, the kind of pestilential bore who makes daily existence
burdensome—office politicians, warring domestic couples, social
climbers, bureaucrats, sycophants and similar nuisances. Whoever
the target, there was invariably a Greek chorus of his co-workers,
relatives, or visitors lounging in the background, commiserating
acidly and hilariously on his shortcomings. Tad had the same
astringent view of his fellow man, the same Pavlovian response to
flim-flam and cant, as that of the great sports commentator Ring
Lardner—doubtless generated in the identical course at ringside
and in the locker room—and as with Lardner, it found its outlet
in slang. It was Tad who coined the phrases, "Yes, we have no
bananas," "23 Skiddoo,", "See what the boys in the back room will
have," "Officer, call a cop," and "Let him up, he's all cut." Among
the apothegms he invented, still part of our common speech, were
such daisies as "The first hundred years are the hardest," "The only
place you'll find sympathy is in the dictionary," and "Half the world
are squirrels and the other half are nuts." Thanks to Tad, insincere
flattery became "applesauce," and pointless gabble "chin music"; his
was the restless, fertile imagination that colored American speech
with terms like "bonehead", "Flat tire", "dumbbell", "lounge lizard",
"cake eater", "finale hopper", "drugstore cowboy", "the once-
over", "the cat's meow", and "for crying out loud". And no matter
what innumerable scholiasts of humor contend, it was to him that
we owe the immortal simile, "As busy as a one-armed paperhanger
with the hives".

   The first of Tad's cartoons to make a dent in my consciousness
were in Hearst's *Boston American* in 1913, and while his art tickled
me, it was not until four years later that his words exerted a profound
effect on my vocabulary. Like every other wide-awake freshman
in my Providence high school, I longed to become a devil with the
ladies, a junior version of such famed Lotharios as Lou Tellegen
and Nat Goodwin, but I realized that I was deficient in repartee.
Somehow a boisterous "Oh, you go on!" and a push never caused

members of the fair sex to collapse in giggles, much less arouse
their lust. There in the balloons overhanging Tad's characters, I
discovered a treasure trove. Overnight my dialogue blossomed out
with nifties like "You tell 'em, goldfish, you've been around the
globe," and "You tell 'em, corset, you've been around the girls."
These , supplemented by a chicken inspector badge that I secreted
under my lapel and flashed with a lewd expression substantially
improved my image. Though no one as yet showed any inclination
to doff her camisole, I received some challenging looks and I felt that
with a bit more practice in winking and leering, I could qualify as
an accomplished roué. About that time, Tad started popularizing his
"I'm the guy" sayings, and I promptly added two socko expressions
to my persiflage. "I'm the guy who put salt in the ocean" and "I'm
the guy who put the pep in pepper." I guess you could say that,
pound for pound , I was just about the most objectionable little
pipsqueak in Rhode Island.

But wait, wait—that was only the beginning! Shortly
thereafter Tad evolved the catch phrase "nobody home" to denote
incomprehension, witlessness, or downright idiocy in those he
was shafting. Daily on the sidelines of his "Indoor Sports" there
appeared one or another of his repertory figures uttering some fresh
orchestration of the idiom, as for instance, "Nobody home but the
oyster and that's in a stew," or 'Nobody home but the flatiron and
that's got a pressing engagement." In a flash, I divined that here
was a whole new dimension for me. I skillfully blended it into my
previous routines, and before long whole rooms would empty at my
approach. My classmates, male and female both, began to display
toward me the sort of revulsion nowadays exclusively reserved for
Alan King. I was, in short, well on my way toward achieving pariah
status, with the result that the school's principal found himself in
a dilemma. What if the entire student body were to boycott the
institution? After all, he could hardly afford to retain a sizable
teaching staff to educate me alone; and being a kindly person, he
decided to put the issue up to me in a one-to-one interview.

"What would you do in my shoes, son?" he inquired. "Suppose it got out that I was running an empty school? Of course, I could tack up scarlatina signs for the time being—"

"Listen, vanilla, don't do me any flavors," I interrupted pertly, and pointed at his distinguished grey temples. "Nobody home but the gas, and that's escaping."

His manner hardened suddenly, and he stood up. "So, wise guy," he snapped. "Stealing from Tad in the *Boston American*, eh? Well, I read him too. As of tomorrow, you're transferred to the Lizzie Borden High School in Fall River, and please convey my heartfelt sympathy to the faculty. Skip the gutter."

And that in a nutshell, is how my life intersected with T.A. Dorgan's—too remotely, I regret, to pay him homage in person for his influence. When he died in 1929, I had been a comic artist for four years for the old *Judge Weekly*, and it doesn't require a residence in psychiatry to understand why I chose that profession. In a generation of brilliant sports cartoonists that included Hype Igoe, Robert Edgren, Burris Jenkins Jr. And Robert Ripley, Tad was acknowledged to be supreme, and those titans of the craft, Milt Gross and Rube Goldberg, were unsparing in their admiration for his guidance and friendship. It was Milt Gross, formerly his office boy on the *New York Evening Journal*, who once imparted a detail about the man that I never forgot. Tad, he said, always worked in a small, bleak office devoid of any pictures or decorations. But lettered on the wall opposite his drawing board was an admonition. It read: "Don't kid yourself."

Cartooon from "Silk Hat Harry's Divorce Suit" and "Indoor Sports" from Schmulowitz Humor Collection, San Francisco History Center, San Francisco Main Public Library. Reprinted by permission.

"How I Learned to Wink and Leer" by S. J. Perelman reprinted by permission of Harold Ober Associates, Inc. **Copyright © 1978 by S.J. Perelman. First published in New York Times Sunday Magazine April 23, 1978**

❧ *Frank Norris*

One street, one man, one view

The street never failed to interest him. It was one of those cross streets peculiar to Western cities, situated in the heart of the residence quarter, but occupied by small trades people who lived in the rooms above their shops. There were corner drug stores with huge jars of red, yellow, and green liquids in their windows, very brave and gay; stationers' stores, where illustrated weeklies were tacked upon bulletin boards; barber shops with cigar stands in their vestibules, sad-looking plumbers' offices, cheap restaurants in whose windows one saw piles of unopened oysters weighted down by cubes of ice, and china pigs and cows knee deep in layers of white beans. At one end of the street McTeague could see the huge powerhouse of the cable line. Immediately opposite him was a great market; while farther on, over the chimney stacks and the intervening houses, the glass roof of some huge public baths glittered like crystal in the afternoon sun. Underneath him the branch post-office was opening its doors, as was the custom between two and three o'clock on Sunday afternoons. An acrid odor of ink rose upward to him. Occasionally a cable car passed, trundling heavily with a strident whirring of jostled glass windows.

On week days the street was very lively. It woke to its work about seven o'clock, at the time when the newsboys made their appearance together with the day laborers. The laborers went trudging past in a straggling file—plumbers' apprentices, their pockets stuffed with sections of lead pipe, tweezers, and pliers; carpenters, carrying nothing but their little pasteboard lunch baskets painted to imitate leather; gangs of street workers, their overalls soiled with yellow clay, their picks and long-handled shovels over their shoulders; plasterers, spotted with lime from head to foot. This little army of workers, tramping steadily in one direction, met and mingled with other toilers of a different description—conductors and 'swing men' of the cable company going on duty; heavy-eyed night clerks from the drug stores on their way home to sleep; roundsmen returning to the precinct police station to make their night report, and Chinese market gardeners teetering past under their heavy baskets. The cable cars began to fill up; all along the street could be seen the shopkeepers taking down their shutters.

Between seven and eight the street breakfasted. Now and then a waiter from one of the cheap restaurants crossed from one sidewalk to the other, balancing on one palm a tray covered with a napkin. Everywhere was the smell of coffee and of frying steaks. A little later, following in the path of the day laborers, came the clerks and shopgirls, dressed with a certain cheap smartness, always in a hurry, glancing apprehensively at the powerhouse clock. Their employers followed an hour or so later—on the cable cars for the most part— whiskered gentlemen with huge stomachs, reading the morning papers with great gravity, bank cashiers and insurance clerks with flowers in their buttonholes.

At the same time the school children invaded the street, filling the air with a clamor of shrill voices stopping at the stationers' shops, or idling a moment in the doorways of the candy stores. For over half an hour they held possession of the sidewalks, then suddenly disappeared, leaving behind one or two stragglers who hurried along with great strides of their little thin legs, very anxious and preoccupied.

Towards eleven o'clock the ladies from the great avenue a block above Polk Street made their appearance, promenading the sidewalks leisurely, deliberately. They were at their morning's marketing. They were handsome women, beautifully dressed. They knew by name their butchers and grocers and vegetable men. From his window McTeague saw them in front of the stalls, gloved and veiled and daintily shod, the subservient provision-men at their elbows scribbling hastily in the order books. They all seemed to know one another, these grand ladies from the fashionable avenue. Meetings took place here and there; a conversation was begun. Others arrived; groups were formed; little impromptu receptions were held before the chopping blocks of butchers' stalls, or on the sidewalk, around boxes of berries and fruit.

From noon to evening the population of the street was of a mixed character. The street was busiest at that time, a vast and prolonged murmur arose—the mingled shuffling of feet, the rattle of wheels, the heavy trundling of cable cars. At four o'clock the school children once more swarmed the sidewalks, again disappearing with surprising suddenness. At six, the great homeward march commenced; the cars were crowded, the laborers thronged the sidewalks, the newsboys chanted the evening papers. Then all at once the street fell quiet; hardly a soul was in sight; the sidewalks were deserted. It was supper hour. Evening began; and one by one a multitude of lights, from the demoniac glare of the druggists' windows to the dazzling blue whiteness of the electric globes, grew thick from street corner to street corner. Once more the street was crowded. Now there was no thought but for amusement. The cable cars were loaded with theatre-goers—men in high hats and young girls in furred opera cloaks. On the sidewalks were groups and couples—the plumbers apprentices, the girls of the ribbon counters, the little families that lived on the second stories over their shops, the dressmakers, the small doctors, the harness-makers—all the various inhabitants of the street were abroad, strolling idly from shop window to shop window, taking the air after the day's work. Groups of girls collected on the corners, talking and laughing very loud, making remarks upon the young men that passed them. The tamale men appeared. A band of Salvationists began to sing before a saloon.

Then, little by little, Polk Street dropped back to solitude. Eleven o'clock struck from the powerhouse clock. Lights were extinguished. At one o'clock the cable stopped, leaving an abrupt silence in the air. All at once it seemed very still. The only noises were the occasional footfalls of a policeman and the persistent calling of ducks and geese in the closed market. The street was asleep.

Frank Norris from MC TEAGUE by Frank Norris, reprinted by permission of Oxford University Press. Frank Norris photo from San Francisco History Center, S.F. Public Library, repinted by permission.

✒ *Isadora Duncan*

Teaching infants (and oneself) a new way to dance.

The character of a child is already plain, even in its mother's womb. Before I was born my mother was in great agony of spirit and in a tragic situation. She could take no food except iced oysters and iced champagne. If people ask me when I began to dance I reply, "In my mother's womb, probably as a result of the oysters and champagne—the food of Aphrodite."

My mother was going through such a tragic experience at this time that she often said, "This child that will be born will surely not be normal," and she expected a monster. And, in fact, from the moment I was born it seemed that I began to agitate my arms and legs in such a fury that my mother cried, "You see, I was quite right; the child is a maniac!" But later on, placed in a baby jumper in the centre of the table, I was the amusement of the entire family and friends, dancing to any music that was played.

My first memory is of a fire. I remember being thrown into the arms of a policeman from an upper window. I must have been about two or three years old, but I distinctly remember the comforting feeling, among all the excitement—the screams and the flames—of the security of the policeman and my little arms around his neck. He must have been an Irishman. I hear my mother crying in her frenzy, "My boys, my boys," and see her held back by the crowd from entering the building in which she imagined my two brothers had been left. Afterwards I remember finding the two boys sitting on the floor of a barroom, putting on their shoes and stockings, and then the inside of a carriage, and then sitting on a counter drinking hot chocolate.

I was born by the sea, and I have noticed that all the great events of my life have taken place by the sea. My first idea of movement, of the dance, certainly came from the rhythm of the waves. I was born under the star of Aphrodite, Aphrodite who was also born on the sea, and when her star is in the ascendant, events are always propitious to me. At these epochs life flows lightly and I am able to create. I have also noticed that the disappearance of this star is usually followed by disaster for me. The science of astrology had not perhaps the importance to-day that it had in the time of the ancient Egyptians or of the Chaldeans, but it is certain that our psychic life is under the influence of the planets, and if parents understood this they would study the stars in the creation of more beautiful children.

I believe, too, that it must make a great difference to a child's life whether it is born by the sea or in the mountains. The sea has always drawn me to it, whereas in the mountains I have a vague feeling of discomfort and a desire to fly. They always give me an impression of being a prisoner to the earth. Looking up at their tops, I do not feel the admiration of the general tourist, but only a desire to leap over them and escape. My life and my Art were born of the sea.

I have to be thankful that when we were young my mother was poor. She could not afford servants or governesses for her children, and it is to this fact that I owe the spontaneous life which I had the opportunity to express as a child and never lost. My mother was a musician and taught music for a living, and as she gave her lessons at the houses of her pupils she was away from home all day and for many hours in the evening. When I could escape from the prison of school, I was free. I could wander alone by the sea and follow my own fantasies. How I pity the children I see constantly attended by nurses and governesses, constantly protected and taken care of and smartly dressed. What chance of life have they? My mother was too busy to think of any dangers which might befall her children, and therefore my two brothers and I were free to follow our own vagabond impulses, which sometimes led us into adventures which, had our mother known of them, would have driven her wild with anxiety. Fortunately she was blissfully unconscious. I say fortunately for me, for it is certainly to this wild, untrammeled life of my childhood that I owe the inspiration of the dance I created, which was but the expression of freedom. I was never subjected to the continual "don'ts" which it seems to me to make children's lives a misery.

I went to the public school at the early age of five. I think my mother prevaricated about my age. It was necessary to have some place to leave me. I believe that whatever one is to do in one's after life is clearly expressed as a baby. I was already a dancer and a revolutionist. My mother, who had been baptized and raised in an Irish Catholic family, was a devout Catholic up to the time when she discovered that my father was not that model of perfection she had always thought him to be. She divorced him, and left with her four children to face the world. From that time her faith in the Catholic religion revolted violently to definite atheism, and she became a follower of Bob Ingersoll, whose works she used to read to us.

Among other things, she decided that all sentimentality was nonsense, and when I was quite a baby she revealed to us the secret of Santa Claus, with the result that at a school festival for Christmas, when the teacher was distributing candies and cakes and said, "See, children, what Santa Claus has brought you," I rose and solemnly replied, "I don't believe you; there is no such thing as Santa Claus."

The teacher was considerably ruffled. "Candies are only for little girls who believe in Santa Claus," she said. "Then I don't want your candy," said I. The teacher unwisely flew into a temper and, to make an example of me, ordered me to come forward and sit on the floor. I came forward and, turning to the class, I made the first of my famous speeches. "I don't believe lies," I shouted. "My mother told me she is too poor to be Santa Claus; it is only the rich mothers who can pretend to be Santa Claus and give presents."

At this the teacher caught hold of me and endeavored to sit me down upon the floor, but I stiffened my legs and held on to her, and she only succeeded in hitting my heels against the parquet. After failing in this, she stood me in the corner, but, although I stood there, I turned my head over my shoulder and shouted, "There is no Santa Claus, there is no Santa Claus," until finally she was forced to send me home. I went home shouting all the way, "There is no Santa Claus," but I never got over the feeling of the injustice with which I had been treated, deprived of candy and punished for telling the truth. When I recounted this to my mother, saying, "Wasn't I right? There is no Santa Claus, is there?" she replied, "There is no Santa Claus and there is no God, only your own spirit to help you." And that night, as I sat upon the rug at her feet, she read us the lectures of Bob Ingersoll.

It seems to me that the general education a child receives at school is absolutely useless. I remember that in the classroom I was either considered amazingly intelligent and at the head of my class, or quite hopelessly stupid and at the bottom of the class. It all depended on a trick of memory, and whether I had taken the trouble to memorize the subject we were given to learn. And I really had not the slightest idea of what it was about. Whether I was at the head or the foot of the class, it was all to me a weary time in which I watched the clock until the hand pointed to three, and we were free. My real education came during the evenings, when my mother played to us Beethoven, Schumann, Schubert, Mozart, Chopin, or read aloud to us from Shakespeare, Shelley, Keats, or Burns. These hours were to us enchanted. My mother recited most of the poetry by heart and I, in imitation of her, one day at a school festival, at the age of

six, electrified my audience by reciting William Lytle's "Antony
to Cleopatra":
   I am dying, Egypt, dying!
   Ebbs the crimson life-tide fast."

On another occasion, when the teacher required of each pupil to
write the history of their lives, my story ran somewhat in this wise:
   "When I was five we had a cottage on 23rd Street. Failing to
pay the rent, we could not remain there, but moved to 17th Street,
and in short time, as funds were low, the landlord objected. So we
moved to 22nd Street, where we were not allowed to leave peacefully
but were moved to 10th Street."

   The history continued in this way, with an infinite number of
removals. When I rose to read it in school, the teacher became very
angry. She thought I was playing a bad joke, and I was sent to the
principal, who sent for my mother. When my poor mother read the
paper she burst into tears and vowed that it was only too true. Such
was our nomadic existence.
   I hope that schools have changed since I was a little girl. My
memory of the teaching of the public schools is that it showed a
brutal incomprehension of children. I also remember the misery of
trying to sit still on a hard bench with an empty stomach, or cold feet
in wet shoes. The teacher appeared to me to be an inhuman monster
who was there to torture us. And of these sufferings children will
never speak.
   I can never remember suffering from our poverty at home,
where we took it as a matter of course; it was only at school that I
suffered. To a proud and sensitive child the public school system, as
I remember it, was as humiliating as a penitentiary. I was always in
revolt against it.
   When I was about six years old, my mother came home
one day and found that I had collected half a dozen babies of the
neighborhood—all of them too young to walk—and had them sitting
before me on the floor while I was teaching them to wave their
arms. When she asked the explanation of this, I informed her that it

was my school of the dance. She was amused, and, placing herself at the piano, she began to play for me. This school continued and became very popular. Later on, little girls of the neighborhood came, and their parents paid me a small sum to teach them. This was the beginning of what afterwards proved a very lucrative occupation.

When I was ten years old the classes were so large that I informed my mother that it was useless for me to go to school any more, as it was only a waste of time when I could be making money, which I considered far more important. I put up my hair on the top of my head and said that I was sixteen. As I was very tall for my age everyone believed me. My sister Elizabeth, who was brought up by our grandmother, afterwards came to live with us and joined in the teaching of these classes. We became in great demand and taught in many houses of the wealthiest people in San Francisco.

As my mother had divorced my father when I was a baby in arms, I had never seen him. Once, when I asked one of my aunts whether I had ever had a father, she replied, "Your father was a demon who ruined your mother's life." After that I always imagined him as a demon in a picture book, with horns and a tail, and when other children at school spoke of their fathers, I kept silent.

When I was seven years old, we were living in two very bare rooms on the third floor, and one day I heard the front doorbell ring, and, on going out into the hall to answer it, I saw a very good-looking gentleman in a top hat, who said:

"Can you direct me to Mrs. Duncan's apartment?"

"I am Mrs. Duncan's little girl," I replied.

"Is this my Princess Pug?" said the strange gentleman. (That had been his name for me when I was a baby.)

And suddenly he took me in his arms and covered me with tears and kisses. I was very much astonished at this proceeding, and asked him who he was. To which he replied with tears, "I am your father."

I was delighted at this piece of news, and rushed in to tell the family.

"There is a man there who says he is my father."

My mother rose, very white and agitated, and, going into the next room, locked the door behind her. One of my brothers hid under the bed and the other retired to a cupboard, while my sister had a violent fit of hysterics.

"Tell him to go away, tell him to go away," they cried.

I was much amazed, but, being a very polite little girl, I went into the hall and said:

"The family are rather indisposed, and cannot receive today," at which the stranger took me by the hand and asked me to come for a walk with him.

We descended the stairs into the street, I trotting by his side in a state of bewildered enchantment to think that this handsome gentleman was my father, and that he had not got horns and a tail, as I had always pictured him.

He took me to an ice-cream parlor and stuffed me with ice cream and cakes. I returned to the family in a state of the wildest excitement and found them in a terribly depressed condition.

"He is a perfectly charming man, and he is coming tomorrow to give me more ice-cream," I told them.'

But the family refused to see him, and after a time he returned to his other family at Los Angeles.

After this I did not see my father for some years, when he suddenly appeared again. This time my mother relented sufficiently to see him, and he presented us with a beautiful house which had large dancing rooms, a tennis court, a barn, and a windmill. This was due to the fact that he had made a fourth fortune. In his life he had made three fortunes and lost them all. This fourth fortune also collapsed in course of time, and with it the house, etc. disappeared. But for a few years we lived in it, and it was a harbor of refuge between two stormy voyages.

Before the collapse I saw my father from time to time, and learned to know that he was a poet, and to appreciate him. Among other poems of his was one which was in a way a prophecy of my entire career.

It was owing to my mother that, as children, our entire lives were permeated with music and poetry. In the evenings she would sit at the piano and play for hours, and there were no set times for rising or going to bed, nor any discipline in our lives. On the contrary, I think my mother quite forgot about us, lost in her music or declaiming poetry, oblivious of all around her. One of her sisters, too, our Aunt Augusta, was remarkably talented. She often visited us and would have performances of private theatricals. She was very beautiful, with black eyes and coal black hair, and I remember her dressed in black velvet "shorts" as Hamlet. She had a beautiful voice, and might have had a great career as a singer had it not been that everything relating to the theater was looked upon by her father and mother as pertaining to the Devil. I realize now how her whole life was ruined by what would be difficult to explain nowadays—the Puritan spirit of America. The early settlers in America brought with them a psychic sense which has never been lost entirely. And their strength of character imposed itself on the wild country, taming the wild men, the Indians, and the wild animals in a remarkable manner. But they were always trying to tame themselves as well, with disastrous results artistically!

From her earliest childhood my Aunt Augusta had been crushed by this Puritan spirit. Her beauty, her spontaneity, her glorious voice, were all annihilated. What was it that made men at that time exclaim, "I would rather see my daughter dead than on the stage?" It is almost impossible to understand this feeling nowadays, when great actors and actresses are admitted to the most exclusive circles.

I suppose it was due to our Irish blood that we children were always in revolt against this Puritanical tyranny.

One of the first effects of our removal to the large house my father gave us was the opening of my brother Augustin's theatre in the barn. I remember he cut a piece out of the fur rug in the parlor to use as a beard for Rip Van Winkle, whom he impersonated in so realistic a manner that I burst into tears as I watched him from a cracker box in the audience. We were all very emotional and refused to be repressed.

The little theatre grew and became quite celebrated in the neighborhood. Later on this gave us kids the idea of making a tournee on the coast. I danced, Augustin recited poems, and afterwards we acted a comedy in which Elizabeth and Raymond also took part. Although I was only twelve years old at the time, and the others still in their teens, these tournees down the coast at Santa Clara, Santa Rosa, Santa Barbara and so forth, were very successful.

The dominant note of my childhood was the constant spirit of revolt against the narrowness of the society in which we lived, against the limitations of life and a growing desire to fly eastward to something I imagined might be broader. How often I remember haranguing the family and my relations, and always ending with, "We must leave this place. We shall never be able to accomplish anything here."

Of all the family I was the most courageous, and, when there was absolutely nothing to eat in the house, I was the volunteer who went to the butcher and through my wiles induced him to give me mutton chops without payment. I was the one sent to the baker to entice him to continue credit. I took a real adventurous pleasure in these excursions, especially when I was successful, as I generally was. I used to dance all the way home with joy, bearing the spoils and feeling like a highwayman. This was a very good education, for, from learning to wheedle ferocious butchers, I gained the technique which enabled me afterwards to face ferocious managers.

I remember once, when I was quite a baby, finding my mother weeping over some things which she had knitted for a shop and which had been refused. I took the basket from her, and, putting one of the knitted caps on my head and a pair of knitted mittens on my hands, I went from door to door and peddled them. I sold everything and brought home twice the money mother would have received from the shop.

When I hear fathers of families saying that they are working to leave a lot of money for their children, I wonder if they realize that by doing so they are taking all the spirit of adventure from the lives of those children. For every dollar they leave them makes them so much the weaker. The finest inheritance you can give to a child is to allow it to make its own way, completely on its own feet. Our teaching led my sister (and me) into the richest houses in San Francisco. I did not envy these rich children; on the contrary, I pitied them. I was amazed at the smallness and stupidity of their lives, and in comparison to these children of millionaires, I seemed to be a thousand times richer in everything that made life worth while.

Our fame as teachers increased. We called it a new system of dancing, but in reality there was no system. I followed my fantasy and improvised, teaching any pretty thing that came into my head. One of my first dances was Longfellow's poem, "I shot an arrow into the air.." I used to recite the poem and teach the children to follow its meaning in gesture and movement. In the evenings my mother played to us while I composed dances. A dear old lady friend who came to spend the evening with us very often, and who had lived in Vienna, said I reminded her of Fanny Elssler, and she would recount to us the triumphs of Fanny Elssler. "Isadora will be a second Fanny Elssler," she would say, and this incited me to ambitious dreams. She told my mother to take me to a famous ballet teacher in San Francisco, but his lessons did not please me. When the teacher told me to stand on my toes I asked him why, and when he replied "Because it is beautiful," I said that it was ugly and against nature, and after the third lesson I left his class, never to return. The stiff and commonplace gymnastics which he called dancing only disturbed my dream. I dreamed of a different dance. I did not know just what it would be, but I was feeling out towards an invisible world into which I divined I might enter if I found the key. My art was already in me when I was a little girl, and it was owing to the heroic and adventurous spirit of my mother that it was not stifled. I believe that whatever the child is going to do in life should be begun when it is very young. I wonder how many parents realize that by the so-called education they are giving their children they are only driving them into the commonplace, and depriving them of any chance of doing anything beautiful or original. But I suppose this must be so, or who would supply us with the thousands of shop and bank clerks, etc., who seem to be necessary for organized civilized life.

My mother had four children. Perhaps by a system of coercion and education she might have turned us into practical citizens and sometimes she lamented, "Why must all four be artists and not one practical?" But it was her own beautiful and restless spirit that made us artists. My mother cared nothing for material things, and she taught us a fine scorn and contempt for all such possessions as houses, furniture, belongings of all kinds. It was owing to her example that I have never worn a jewel in my life. She taught us that such things were trammels.

When they reached San Francisco, my grandfather built one of the first wooden houses, and I remember visiting this house when I was a little girl, and my grandmother, thinking of Ireland, used often to sing the Irish songs and dance the Irish jigs, only I fancy that into these Irish jigs had crept some of the heroic spirit of the pioneer and the battle with the Redskins—probably some of the gestures of the Redskins themselves, and, again a bit of Yankee Doodle, when Grandfather Colonel Thomas Gray came marching home from the Civil War. All this grandmother danced in the Irish jig, and I learnt it from her, putting into it my own aspiration of Young America, and, finally, my great spiritual realization of life from the lines of Walt Whitman. And that is the origin of the so-called Greek dance with which I have flooded the world.

That was the origin—the root—but afterwards, coming to Europe, I had three great masters, the three great precursors of the dance of our century—Beethoven, Nietzsche, and Wagner. Beethoven created the dance in mighty rhythm. Wagner in sculptural form, Nietzsche in sprit. Nietzsche was the first dancing philosopher.

Why should our children bend the knee in that fastidious and servile dance, the minuet, or twirl in the mazes of the false sentimentality of the waltz? Rather let them come forth with great strides, leaps and bounds, with lifted forehead and far-spread arms, to dance the language of our pioneers, the fortitude of our heroes, the justice, kindness, purity of our statesmen, and all the inspired love and tenderness of our mothers. When the American children dance in this way, it will make of them beautiful beings, worthy of the name of the Greatest Democracy.

That will be America dancing.

🪶 *James J. Corbett*

Learning to fight, then learning to box

From my first fight I started to run away. This scrap came at an early age, when I was about twelve years old. I was attending St. Ignatius College in San Francisco, and at noon and recess periods was confined to what they called the "Little Yard". Up to a certain grade you were in the "Little Yard" with the smaller youngsters, and when you were promoted out of the "Little Yard" you could go in the "Big Yard" with the big boys; but I was always large for my age and looked much older than I really was, so I would go to the picnics and they would have prizes for boys under twelve years old and they never would let me try for them, and I felt rather out of it and often lonely, so whenever I could I would sneak in the "Big Yard" at lunch times to play handball and prisoners' base with the older boys.

The bully of the "Big Yard" was a boy called "Fatty" Carney, but I had never been warned about him. Now about this time I struck up an acquaintance with a fellow by the name of Hopkins. We used to bring our own lunches, as we lived quite a distance from the school, and this Hopkins boy, whose folks were well-to-do, brought all the finest kinds of cakes and sandwiches. Perhaps this was one of the attractions of the friendship. Anyway, I used to go in and play with him and get some of his lunch which was much finer than anything I had ever had. In playing prisoners' base one day I happened to chase him, and "Fatty" Carney the bully I have just spoken of, was running after someone else and Hopkins ran into "Fatty" and Carney promptly hit him. Of course I took Hopkins' part, as he was my pal and grabbed Carney's arms and started to fight him then and there, but the other boys interfered and a Brother of the College came and ordered me back to the "Little Yard" where I belonged, but not before Carney had said, "I'll get you after school!" Someone was then kind enough to inform me that I was up against the toughest fellow in the school.

When school was dismissed that afternoon one of the boys whispered to me, as we marched out in line, that Carney was waiting for me outside. My first intention was to run away. There were two exits and I was trying to decide which was the safer when it suddenly occurred to me that if I ran away all the boys would laugh at me and I would be looked upon as a coward. I kept thinking it over while I was marching but my pride was now aroused and I said to myself, "I will go out and get licked." And out I marched on the street and there was Carney with a bunch of fellows surrounding him, waiting. I was only a kid then. But that afternoon an idea came to me that has since stood me in good stead—to avoid trouble, if possible, but if it lay ahead of me, to be the aggressor and not let the other fellow think I was at all afraid. In my heart I was afraid of Carney then but I marched right over to him, scared as I was, and said, "Are you waiting for me?" He said "Yes."

We went around to a lot opposite the United States Mint called the "Mint Yard", and the whole school followed. We started to fight. He was a big strong fellow—if we had been men and in a regular ring, they would have called him the slugger, and me a panther, terms much used in descriptions of fights those days.

I had never had a boxing lesson, but occasionally had watched my older brother box. He was six years older than I and I remembered a few of his tricks, such as looking at the stomach and hitting in the face--just the crude principles of the boxing art.

Fatty started to rush me, and as he was stronger and older than I, I began to jump out of his way, trying to make him miss. Then I'd jab at him and jump away—instinctively using my head even at that age, though I didn't realize it myself. After a few minutes the police came and scattered us, but by that time I was sure I could whip Fatty, and when we ran away from the police, I ran in the same direction that he took, as I wanted to have it out with him. He made for his home, and we came to the "Circus Lot", used for the circus performances in those days. I had no supporters with me, just two or three of the boys of my own neighborhood who had followed me, while Fatty had his whole gang at his back. We started fighting in this lot and I was getting the better of him and he realized it, so he grabbed hold of me and started to wrestle and, being much stronger than I, threw me down and proceeded to punch me while I lay underneath him. An old gentleman, with a cane, stood near, watching us. He took the cane in his hand and stepped in and hit Fatty on the back with it and told him he ought to fight boys of his own age and size. I went home with a black eye.

My father, an old-fashioned Irishman, discovered this little souvenir of the fight. Pointing to it, he asked sternly, "Where did you get this?"

I explained the circumstances to him and told him it had been a case of either fighting or running away and being called a coward. I didn't realize at the time that my father was really proud of me because I had not chosen the other entrance of the school. He asked me who it was I had fought with and I told him Fatty Carney.

"Carney down on Howard Street?" He asked.

In those days San Francisco wasn't as big as it is now and everybody knew everybody else, And he repeated, "Carney down on Howard Street? H'm,! What d'ye think of that!" He seemed surprised to think that I had been fighting with this big Carney boy and couldn't understand it.

I returned to school the next day; so did Carney. Then the older boys in the "Big Yard" came around, making a fuss over me, and I could hear the boys talking and saying to each other, "Why you ought to have seen him yesterday! This kid was shifting and using judgment just the way professionals do."

I was surprised and pleased, but the wind was taken out of my sails when the head of the College appeared and put us both out of school. He did not suspend us, but expelled us for good. Anyway, this fight grew to be a legend, a sort of historical event in the school and was talked of long afterwards, so the boys told me.

From that fight I learned a lesson that has lasted me all my life—that the size of a man does not count. And that by using my head and feet I could lick a man much stronger than myself.

I don't think that I really proved that I had what I call real courage in that first fight. After all, it was merely a question of my pride. As a matter of fact, I do not think I had my courage tested until eight years afterwards when I fought [Joe] Choinyski. Then I found out what it means to keep on going in the face of a terrible beating, when defeat stares you in the face.

The next year I attended Sacred Heart College. Two incidents of that year stand out in my mind. There was a boy from my neighborhood who went to this school and who was subject to epileptic fits. He used to look on me as a protector. When one of those attacks would come on the teacher would say, "Corbett, take him out into the yard." Out we would go, and when the attack subsided we would have a real good time together. This gave me a bright idea, and finally one day I tried it. I leaned over to my epileptic friend and whispered, "Tim, can you throw a fit for me?"

Being grateful for all my trouble he did this promptly as a little act of friendship. The teacher yelled, "Corbett, take him out!" and we had a wonderful time, fooling around playing knife and telling stories, and stayed out in the yard about an hour. This worked so splendidly that we tried it at least once a week and got many an unearned recess thereby.

During this period I had some fights. I think I can truthfully say that I never started one. In fact I have tried to follow such a policy all my life; but after the first fight with Carney, through the confidence gained in it, I never took any back talk from any boy, no matter what his size.

The second incident that I recall most vividly was quite dramatic and was also the cause of my being expelled from Sacred Heart College.

One of the boys sitting behind me was constantly whispering slurs at me. This I, of course, resented. The Brother in charge of the classroom called me forward, broke a window pole in half, told me to hold out my hand, and gave me one of the most terrific blows I have ever had in my life. The pain was intense and when he said "Hold out your other hand," for once I didn't obey, and turned and walked back to my seat.

When the class was dismissed I started to go out with the other boys but was ordered by this kindhearted Brother to remain behind the rest. I caught a glimpse of the big stick under his gown, and lit out of the door. This happened to be on the fourth floor, and the school was so built that there were four galleries circling an open court. Around each successive gallery I ran, pursued by the brother with this stick, then on the third floor by two or more of the order, on the second by another group, until I came to the bottom where a seventh lay in wait—a big fat fellow looking like Friar Tuck. I have heard since of the "solar plexus blow." It was not then known, but I delivered it—with my head—in the fat Brother's stomach and over we went, rolling on the floor and out into the street. This valedictory ended my schooldays, though not my education.

School over, work was ahead. My father kept a livery stable and among his customers was the cashier of the Nevada Bank of San Francisco, J.S. Angus. One of the owners of this bank was John W. Mackay, father of the well known Clarence H. Mackay. Mr. Angus got me a job as messenger boy and I worked there for six years, rising at last to the post of assistant receiving teller.

During this period from 1879-1886—I used to box frequently. With my father's consent, I kept boxing gloves in the stable, and the boys of the neighborhood would come around in the evenings after supper, and we had many informal bouts.

However, the form of athletics that seemed to appeal to me most at this time was baseball. In fact I think I may say that I was headed for the Big League, for our team, "The Alcazars," played against clubs that had on their rosters such players as Ed Morris and Fred Carroll, later a famous battery of the Pittsburgh Nationals, George Van Haltren, for many years center fielder of the Giants, Tom Brown of the Washingtons, and many others that figured in the box scores of the '80s and '90s. With those whose names I have just mentioned, and others who later became famous, I was really being groomed by the baseball magnates of the Coast for a baseball career.

There is a famous story called "A Piece of String," which tells of a man who stooped down to pick up this little article and so had his whole career changed. Well, that is what a simple thing like a liner did for me—it split my hand between the little and third fingers so badly that I had to leave the diamond, and thereafter devoted more time to boxing.

Just before this accident occurred I had been asked by the officers of the famous Olympic Athletic Club of San Francisco to play second base for their team. Unfortunately I never did, because of the mishap just referred to, but it brought me within the walls of this club, famous in all sporting annals, and there I began to take up boxing in a more serious way.

At this time I had a pal named Lew Harding who was interested in boxing and still more so in wrestling. In his father's cellar he had boxing gloves and a wrestling pad, and twice a week we went to this favorite haunt at night. Now his ideas about training were not as helpful as his ideas of wrestling. As soon as we arrived as first part of our routine we would freeze four quarts of ice cream. When that was hard, we would wrestle half an hour, then eat a quart of cream, following this up with boxing for an hour; after which strenuous exercise we would eat up the remainder of the cream. It was enough to kill any ordinary individual and I would not advise anyone seriously considering taking up boxing adopting this course.

I did not really know that I had any natural boxing ability, although I had tried to remember and put in practice certain things I had seen professionals do; however, Lew saw in me things that I didn't see in myself—quickness of eye and feet, and a natural understanding of and instinct for the game. So without telling me that he was putting me through a course of stunts for any purpose he began to take me around to various places where I must "mix it" with the toughest characters in town.

For instance, on Wednesday nights he would lead me, an unconscious victim, to the fire engine house where the roughest young fellows of the town used to congregate, and on Friday nights to a blacksmith shop where the crowd was even worse. I had a good many fights at each of these places—some of them pretty tough ones, for as I said, the gangs were composed of noted scrappers of the town. When I first came there they used to sneer at me and look upon me as a "dude", for, being a bank clerk, I naturally took pains with my personal appearance. However, I fought myself into their estimation and soon they forgot to call me this withering name and made no more remarks about my white collar or kid gloves, although many compliments were paid me about my use of those of another sort.

By and by, having licked all the regular frequenters of the place, they began to scout around along the shore front, The Barbary Coast, and all the low dives of the underworld to secure the roughest talent they could. I found the road pretty tough going for a while, but stuck it out, never losing a single bout. All these were earned without any real boxing instruction, which was to come later; but here I feel I developed resourcefulness, generalship, and ability to size up all kinds of men. Of course, my antagonists were all of the brutal slugging type, and used no judgment at all; but it was undoubtedly a great experience for me.

When I joined the Olympic Club it happened that their building had just burned down and the members were using the Turn Verein, which had an open gymnasium, a gallery and a running track. The first day after I had signed up, being very confident of my ability, through my victories in the engine house and blacksmith shop, I went up to the boxing instructor to take him on. He asked me if I had ever boxed and I replied, with a great deal of pride, "Oh yes, hundreds of times!" He said, "Box with me a while," and then proceeded to show me up.

It seems that in the gallery were several German friends of his and he tried to make a monkey out of this fresh kid to their great delight. Every time my head went back from one of his blows they would roar over their steins until the rafters rang. He hit me so often that I thought there was a shower of boxing gloves like big hailstones coming through the air. Although I had always managed to keep good control of my temper, I felt that afternoon that he, with his skill, was taking advantage of a youngster in rather a mean way and showing off before his German friends. I saw red and began to rough it with him, scuffling around, and he threatened to report me and have my privileges at the club rescinded. So that ended our relations.

The next day my friend Harding and I went to the club again and I saw a fellow with an immense black beard like a Russian's or the ones the bearded miners wore in '48. (There were still some left around Frisco.) Blackbeard was boxing with a friend and he must have been fooling with him, but I didn't know this at the time. He had a magnificent torso, like Jeffries', but I didn't take note of it just then; all I could see were those black whiskers, and I said to myself, "A fellow who would wear a beard like that cannot box."

Then I leaned over to my friend Harding and suggested that he fix it up for me. Harding went over to the Professor and asked him to arrange a few rounds with the black-bearded man. The Professor smiled, seeing revenge ahead, as this fellow, although I did not know it, was the heavyweight champion of the club, weighed 215 pounds, and was a terrific hitter.

The gloves once on, I struck out for the black-beard—for still all I could see were those whiskers. In the next second I was sitting in a chair and they were throwing water over me, rubbing my legs and holding smelling salts to my nose. I had been knocked dead cold, but even then didn't realize it.

I got up and, in a groggy way, said, "Come on, let's box," but Blackbeard replied:

"No, you have had enough for today."

To show them that I was all right and had not been hurt I started to circle the running track, which ran around the room, the center being occupied by the apparatus. Somehow I couldn't keep to the track and before I had lurched three yards was reeling into the center of the room and banging into the apparatus, still very groggy and in danger of other knockout blows—from the parallel bars and flying rings.

Lew led me from the gymnasium down to the dressing room, and then it began to dawn on me that I had really been knocked out and for the first time in my life; and I think it was one of the greatest blows to my pride I have ever experienced. I saw then that I needed boxing instruction.

About twelve months after this incident the beautiful new Olympic Club was opened and a boxing instructor, Walter Watson, was imported from England. On the first day of his appearance a man named Eiseman, who happened to be the middleweight champion of the club, asked Watson for a bout, and in front of his [Eiseman's] friends tried to put the finishing touch on the new teacher, a grandstand, and very mean trick, also decidedly unethical, as Eiseman was a younger man than Watson and the latter was not in condition and was simply engaged to teach the members points. There followed a terrific fight which was later stopped, and Watson, resenting the unfairness of it, shook his fist in Eiseman's face and said, "In three months I will develop some youngster from this club who will give you the worst licking you ever had in your life."

The next day, I, being sixth on the list for the boxing lesson, waited my turn with the instructor. Meantime, I watched the other men and noticed that they all seemed afraid of Watson and didn't open up. This caution—or respect—rather annoyed him, I also noticed, because he was anxious to find out how much they knew and what material he had to work with. When it came to my turn he asked me, "Have you ever boxed?"

"A good many times," I told him.

He said, "Open up; I want you to show me what you have."

Feeling a little impressed by this man, who was quite noted for his skill, I looked at him, puzzled, and inquired, "Do you really mean it?" "Of course," he replied, impatiently.

"Open up with all I have and hit you as hard as I want to?" I asked, to make sure. He smiled, "That's what I want."

So off I started, like a runaway horse, and showered blows at him from all directions. In about a minute he held up his hand and said, "Is there any Irish blood in you, by any chance?" "Yes, sir, my father and mother are Irish," I answered.

He grinned. "In three months you will lick any man in this club."

His confidence somehow seemed to stimulate me as no other words had ever done. Every spare moment I could get I practiced feints and shifts, even trying them before my mirror at night, and in the morning would study my own action, which furnished considerable amusement for my other brothers who looked through the door. Meanwhile the instructor took particular pains with me from then on and I became his favorite pupil.

After I had taken my second boxing lesson I approached my brother Harry, who was next to the oldest of the ten children in our family, and asked him to put on the gloves with me. Having always been able to cuff me about as he liked, he laughed at me, but I persisted and finally, giving in, he went out to the box stall in the livery stable.

A little patronizingly he put up his hands, but before he knew it I had hit him so quickly that he was jolted hard up against the sides of the stall. This was a new experience for him and he grew angry and started to rush me; but I had benefitted by my lessons and shifted and ducked this way and that under his arm so he couldn't land a glove on me. I tried one or two more blows on him; then he suddenly stopped and said, with a mischievous grin, "Wait! I'll get Frank!"

Now Frank was my oldest brother and had always had a wonderful time chasing me about and was considered the star scrapper of the family. Harry found him and he came into the box stall, all confidence and prepared to give me the punishment earned by my freshness and impudence. Like Harry he put his hands up, but before he had time even to lead I had landed at least ten blows on him in such rapid succession that he was quite as stunned as Harry had been. I was under him and back of him and all around; he might as well have been chasing a shadow, and then I turned to and slammed him all over the place. He tore off the gloves and went into the office of the livery stable where my father sat, busy at his accounts.

"Dad," said Frank, "You better look out for that fellow."

Watching by the window, I heard Dad reply, without discontinuing his work, "What fellow?"

"Jim."

Then he looked up.

"Why, what has he done?"

"Done!" exclaimed Frank, "why he's just knocked Harry and me all over the box stall out there and he'll turn into a prizefighter if you don't look out, he's getting so chesty!"

The old gentleman laughed and thought it was a great joke, but of course didn't take it seriously.

As you may have guessed, we were a very united family, but naturally, like all others, had our troubles, and one of the things that impressed me most, even as a boy was hearing my father and mother, who were quite thrifty, talking about that mortgage of $6,000 on their San Francisco home and the stable property. You see that although he worked hard, his livery stable business could not bring many luxuries to a family of twelve.

During the time I held the position in the bank, I used to keep his books at night to help him out and realized just how he stood and was early impressed with his financial hardships. Seeing him worry about the feed bill and all such little details brought this home, and then and there, even as a boy, I determined if I ever got hold of any big sum of money, the first thing I would do would be to pay off that mortgage. Then, if there was anything left, I planned to send them to the old country to see their childhood home. Often they used to talk about the place and say, "Oh, if we could only see Ireland again before we die!"

A fellow never had better or more affectionate parents than I. Perhaps they were a little too lenient with us sometimes, but I think on the whole they were just. Honestly, I cannot think, as I look back over the years, of a single mistake they ever made, except perhaps in being too open-hearted. For instance, I can now remember how once, after I became champion and was playing in San Francisco, my mother insisted on having the whole company of forty people out to see her, simply because "they were friends of Jim's." And I know they never tasted a better supper, and after it was over my sister went to the piano and accompanied my mother singing "Annie Laurie" in her sweet old voice. When the song was over Father and Mother, in response to a unanimous demand, danced an Irish jig. She was a beautiful waltzer, too—so light on her feet, although she was plump. I have never danced with a finer, it seems to me.

That there was harmony in our family, and respect paid to our parents, is evident from the fact that for the six years I was a bank clerk I gave my monthly salary to my mother each payday. Afterwards I would ask my father for what I needed from time to time. When my mother died they found in her bureau a bank book in my name with the entries of my salary, the first of each month, showing the raises as they came along.

Their plans for me may seem amusing to some of my friends for earlier in life they had determined upon my being a priest— perhaps because a brother of my father's, who was born after father left Ireland and whom he had never seen, the uncle for whom I was named, was a priest.

❧ *Carl Nolte*

If you don't call it Frisco, then what do you call it?

If you have spent any time in bookstores lately, you must have noticed that there are books on San Francisco's past, present and future: books that tell you where to drink, where to drive, where to take a bus, where to stay, what to look at and even how to cook in the San Francisco style, whatever that is. But no book tells you how to act like a native San Franciscan, because it is widely assumed that the breed, if it ever existed, is extinct.

One book, *San Francisco Free and Easy,* subtitled "The Native's Guide Book," says on the first page, "San Franciscans are notorious newcomers. You'll find few people here with the sort of roots common to East Coast cities." Another, written by a carpetbagger named John K. Bailey is called *The San Francisco*

Insider's Guide. It begins, "On my first visit to San Francisco, 15 years ago…"

Fifteen years ago? I know a cat who's lived here longer than that. A terrible thing has happened to native San Franciscans. They have become strangers in their own city. Their whole culture is in danger of being swallowed up by foreigners from New York, Ohio, New Hampshire, Denver, and other places Back East. These newcomers all assume everyone else is a newcomer. The first thing to go is the language. Despite everything you've ever heard, there is a distinctive San Francisco way of talking and it is important to make note of it, for the record, before it becomes as dead as Latin. Here's how to talk like a San Franciscan.

The first lesson-learned at birth-is never to call it Frisco or San FRANcisco. Most resident tourists have settled on something that sounds liked an Anglicized version of the Spanish San Francisco, but natives run the two words together and add a couple of extra sounds, and it comes out "Sampencisco." It may also be called thecity, which is one word. It is never called The City, which is two words and tacky.

One way to tell San Franciscans is the way they run words together. Another way is that all native San Franciscans know something about other native San Franciscans. This cannot be faked. The first test comes when a native San Franciscan is introduced to someone he does not know at a party. Sooner or later, one will ask the other where he or she is from. The correct dialogue goes like this:

Q: Whereya from?

A: Here.

Q: Oh yeah? Whereja go to school?

A: Poly.

Q: Oh yeah? Doyaknow (fill in name of acquaintance)?

At once, the two people realize they are both natives and doubtless have friends, experiences, and a whole subculture in common.

There are several keys to this small bit of conversation.

First, the true native runs all the words together. He never says, "Where are you from?" because that is the way they talk Back East. When he asks where you went to school, he means high school-not college, not trade school, and certainly not P.S. 178.

The correct answer is one of several San Francisco high schools. "Poly," of course means Polytechnic High School, which not only reveals your high school but what district of the city you came from, and other details.

If, for example, the answer is "S.I.", you know the man went to St. Ignatius High, and was probably raised a Catholic and is from an upper-middle-class family. SH people were from North Beach and the Mission, better known as Sacred Heart.

If the person says "Mission" or "Bal" (for Balboa High) you know he is from the Mission District, and his father was probably a member of the working class, called "a workin' man" in the San Francisco dialect.

If he went to Lowell, he may well be Jewish; if he went to Galileo, he is probably a North Beach Italian, and not a Mission District Italian.

One has to be careful, though. Some women, asked where they went to school, will respond that they "went to the madams." A tourist will immediately leap to the conclusion that the poor woman was raised in a whorehouse, but natives understand immediately what this woman means: She attended the Convent of the Sacred Heart, conducted by a ritzy order of nuns, and is doubtless from a wealthy family. She is not necessarily a Catholic, however. Diane Feinstein went to the madams.

The next thing to note about this conversation is that the proper response to a remark is "Yeah?" not " You don't say so?" or "Is that right?" San Franciscans say "yeah" a lot, but it doesn't always mean yes.

Now you are ready for your geography lesson. Oakland, Berkeley, and all those other places are "across the Bay." The largest city in Santa Clara County is " Sannazay," not "San Jose". Sannazay is near "Sannacruise". To get there, you have to go Down the Peninsula, past South City, Sammateo, Rewoodcity and a whole buncha other towns.

The River is the Russian River and no other, but the Lake is Lake Tahoe only if your family was wealthy; otherwise the lake is Clear Lake. The Mountain is Tamalpais; Mount Diablo is "Dyeaablo" and has no first name.

The town on the river is called Gurneyville, even though the correct pronunciation is Gurnville. San Franciscans know the correct pronunciation but choose not to use it. If corrected on this, a native will likely say, "If those guys up there are so smart, what'er they doin' livin' there? People who live in Gurneyville all year are a buncha Okies anyway." It should be noted that being called an Okie—as in persons from Oklahoma or anywhere south is among the worst insults a San Franciscan can offer; it means a person lacks taste or sophistication.

Natives are often asked for directions, sometimes by tourists and often by pseudo-natives. A San Franciscan of course has no idea where anything across the Bay is, but he knows all about San Francisco.

To start with, unless a street is tiny, like Saturn Street or Macondray Lane, it is never called by its full name. You never say "Taraval Street," for example, only "Taraval." When you direct someone to go "out Geary," by which is meant you go west. You know, toward the beach. One never goes "in Mission," or "in Geary." To head in the general direction of downtown, one goes "down Mission" or "down Geary."

It is "the beach," too, not the seashore or the coast. The coast is Down the Peninsula, near Sharp Park. There are no beaches on the Bay, despite evidence to the contrary-only on the ocean.

San Franciscans know there are 30 numbered streets and 48 avenues; they know Arguello is First Avenue and Funston is 13th Avenue. They know that First Street is not the first street, and that Main is not the main street.

The Richmond district is always called "The Richmond," and the Sunset District is always called "The Sunset," but Noe Valley has no article in front of its name; neither does downtown or North Beach. No one knows why.

Natives do know it is always 24th (pronounced twenny fourth) and Mission, not Mission and 24th. It's Second and Clement, not Clement and Second. The street is not pronounced "CLEment" but "CleMENT.'

There is no need to make a distinction between Second Street and Second Avenue in this case, since San Franciscans know that Second Street and Clement do not intersect. They know several other things, too: that Alcatraz is not called The Rock, that Yerba Buena Island is called Goat Island or YBI, that French bread is not called sourdough bread and never was. The name "sourdough" for honest bread was invented by advertising guys from Chicago or someplace.

They know that Italians do not eat pizza. They eat spaghetti, tagliarini, or some other stuff, mostly in North Beach, but sometimes in small places in the Mission or Daly City. Daly City is near the county line. San Francisco has no city limit.

San Franciscans call the movie theatre "the show," as in "I went to the show last week, and jeez, the guy behind me was coffin all through the pitcher. I couldn' hardly stant it" "The theatre (pronounced "thee-ater") refers to the legitimate stage.

There are San Francisco threats, too. One of the worst is to act so irresponsibly that you will be put away, as in "if you keep actin' like that, you'll end up in Napa," which, of course, is the local mental hospital. This threat has lost some of its power lately, since these days half the people at Powell & Market appear to be deranged.

Another threat is the danger of being forsaken by your family and friends in your old age and sent to Laguna Honda, the city's old folks' home.

When San Franciscans read papers, they read the Ex (the *Examiner*) or the *Chronicle* (never called the Chron) Old guys usta read the Call (as the *Call-Bulletin* was called) or the Noos (the *San Francisco News*, which very old residents called the Dailynoos). San Franciscans never, ever read the *San Francisco Magazine*, which is written, edited, and produced for tourists.

Television is pretty much a wasteland of standard spoken English, though there are a few bright spots. Joe Di Maggio, a native of Martinez who was raised in North Beach, sometimes appears on behalf of a product he calls "Mista CAWfee", and it is possible to watch the news on KPIX, because anchorman Dave McElhatton is suspected of being a native, or, on KGO, where Van Amburg holds forth. He went to State, ya know.

With any luck, you might catch Russ Couglin, also on KGO-TV. He is a graduate of Mission High, and has the last pure San Francisco accent on the local airwaves.

As for the rest, it's pretty hard to hear all these radio and TV types mispronounce the names we all grew up with ("I'm standing here at the Persiddio" or "at Mare Island, up by Valley-jo." Or, as I heard last week, "He was buried in Colima."

Most of us grew up under the delusion that everybody was a native San Franciscan. It was the largest small town in the world, and we thought it the only city that counted. Occasional tourists complimented us on the city, but we never dreamed they'd move here and take over. Everywhere else was far away, and the jet plane hadn't been invented. I went to high school with a guy who was a direct descendant of Francisco De Haro, the first alcalde of Yerba Buena, and I have a friend whose great-great grandfather walked to California from Rabbit Hash, Ky. In 1855. No big deal.

Once, after she bought a house in the Richmond, one of her new neighbors asked her where she was from. "I moved out here six months ago," she said. "Oh, from the East or Midwest?" the neighbor asked. "No," she said, "from California and Buchanan."

Perhaps you are now thinking of fooling your friends by pretending to be a native. Don't try. There is only one way to be a native San Franciscan. You gotta be born here.

"Anybody," my grandfather used to say, "can be born in Oakland, or Back East. It's an honor to be born in Sampencisco."

"How to Speak like a San Franciscan" by Carl Nolte originally appeared in the *San Francisco Chronicle* and has been circulating on email and websites ever since. Reprinted by permission of The Hearst Corporation. Photograph of Carl Nolte courtesy of Carl Nolte.

🌿 *Anita Loos*

The Barbary Coast: in life and in film.

In that era the tenderloin of San Francisco, famous as the Barbary Coast, was in full flower. The district extended for about five blocks, a dazzling area of cafes, gambling spots, honkytonks, and places for more lusty diversion. Possibly its name had been invented by some world traveler who thought it resembled a certain wicked quarter on the Berber Coast. But sin in San Francisco had a special quality; the Barbary Coast developed its own brand of entertainment and copied no other place. Its honkytonks and sporting houses welcomed colored musicians at a time when they were barred from most white places, so San Francisco heard ragtime at its beginning; appreciated, fostered, and developed it. The raciest of American slang was invented on the Barbary Coast, much of it by an outrageous young man named Wilson Mizner. Generations

yet to come will be quoting Mizner without ever having heard his
name, although H.L. Mencken's treatise, *The American Language*,
bestows full credit on him. It is difficult to give a true impression
of Mizner's wit on paper because a great deal of it seems violent
to the point of bad taste. But Mizner was no roughneck; he was a
gentleman; he was even a "dude". He sent to London for his clothes
at a period when such foppery was unheard of in the uncouth West.
He was also a man of breeding: the Mizners were direct descendants
of Sir Joshua Reynolds, and Wilson's father was an ambassador from
the United States to some South American country. Above all, he
was extremely handsome; not only did these facts absolve Wilson's
humor of vulgarity, but they gave it a unique shock value. To hear
that imposing and elegant creature come out with a statement such
as one he made about Hollywood during the Fatty Arbuckle scandal
produced a rather special effect.

"Living in Hollywood," said Wilson, "is like floating down a
sewer in a glass-bottom boat."

The burlesque theatres of the Barbary Coast developed
several artists who became stars on Broadway; one of them was
Blossom Seeley. She appeared on television not so long ago, a
sprightly old lady who delivered some of her early song-and-dance
numbers belonging to the period of the Bunny Hug. But the most
distinguished star to emerge from the Coast was David Warfield.
He toured America for years with a serio-comedy called *The Music
Master* in which he played an old Austrian piano teacher. There was
one moment in the last act when Warfield reduced his audience to
audible sobs It came in a scene where the Music Master was called
on to protect a young girl who was being disowned by her parents;
"If you don't need her, I need her," the old Austrian declared. "If
you don't vant her, *I* vant her!" In time, that speech became a catch
phrase and a joke, but David Warfield's performance has remained
a classic in the annals of the American Theater. There is no record
of where Warfield worked on the Barbary Coast, but the only
spot that featured "legitimate" acting was a tiny theatre where the
drawing-room comedies of Sir Arthur Wing Pinero were acted quite
earnestly except that the performers didn't wear any clothes. So

the eminent old thespian may have been trained in that naughty and irreverent troupe.

As youngsters we had a lively curiosity about the Barbary Coast, but I was never to see it, for if we children wandered in that neighborhood we were quickly turned back by the first passer-by. But when I was writing scenarios at M.G.M., I collaborated on a movie about the Barbary Coast with one of the studio's staff writers, Bob Hopkins. "Hoppy" had been a messenger boy on the Coast in its heyday, when Wilson Mizner was a young dandy in silk hat, white tie, and tails, who gambled with rich suckers for big stakes. Our movie was called *San Francisco;* its leading character was inspired by Wilson Mizner and played by Clark Gable, whose performance suggested much of Wilson's insouciance and illicit charm. Costarring with Gable were Jeanette MacDonald and Spencer Tracy, and the film has often been televised on the Late Late Show.

A chain of fond associations developed during the making of that movie. Three of us had the sentimental bond of being fellow San Franciscans. Herb Nacio Brown, who composed some of its song numbers, had played piano as a youth in a honkytonk on the Barbary Coast. Our theme song, "San Francisco", was selected by a competition among the composers under contract at M.G.M. and won by a young Bronislaw Kaper, who had just arrived from Yugoslavia, spoke little English and had never seen the place that was supposed to be his inspiration. However, Broni's tune so characterized the brisk spirit of San Francisco that it was adopted as a theme song by the city itself. Herb Brown wrote many more important melodies than the ones he composed for our movie, among them " Singing in the Rain"; and Broni was responsible for the score of the film *Lili,* with its enchanting "Hi Lili, Hi Lili, Hi Low," but I doubt if any of us have ever had more fun than during the sessions when Herb or Broni was at the piano and Hoppy and I doped out the plot of *San Francisco.*

My Pop's exciting girl friends must have caused Mother many hours of suffering. But when troubled she kept her mouth shut as did her own mamma. Pop never heard a word of complaint and, until I reached an age for snooping, I myself was unaware of his infidelities I was first to hear about them one afternoon when a strange young woman showed up at the house to pay a call on Mother; She was the type now termed a "dish," and I remember she wore a tailored suit of baby-blue linen combined with an oversized white lace jabot and a big bright red hat Her chic appearance made me curious and I tiptoed to the door to listen. It appeared that she had come with a plea for my mother to get an immediate divorce and let her have R. Beers [R.Beers Loos, her father] for keeps But instead of treating the beauty with disdain my mother was actually sympathetic. She explained that she had suffered for years because of other women's infatuation with her Harry, and that it would be best for the young lady to be assured of his feelings before trying to legalize her penchant for him. The beauty who had prepared herself for a big dramatic scene, was so let down by Mother's composure that she couldn't find adequate dialogue for it. She departed and presumably went the way of all the young creatures who threatened to disrupt our home.

My childish reaction to finding out this new dimension of Pop's charm was rather along the same lines as Mother's. I realized the situation to be sad, but I didn't hold Pop accountable. How could he be blamed because fascinating ladies fell in love with him? In fact, I sometimes wondered how anyone so lacking in spirit as my mother had ever managed to hook my scintillating Pop.

In due course Pop's extravagances undermined *The Dramatic Review* and it passed out of existence, even while his reputation as a humorist was on the increase through his being quoted in other periodicals. By that time, however, Pop had become more than content to ad-lib his jokes to an admiring audience while standing with one foot on the rail of a bar.

Presently the Loos family started moving from one district of San Francisco to another on a descending scale of prosperity. Mother always refused to write home for money, except when our needs became acute. I figure that Grandpa had a pretty depressing way of letting her know "I told you so." Luckily, however, we had

stumbled onto two new sources of income. Mother began to take in
roomers and Gladys and I were put to work as actresses.

Our professional careers, however, were due to Pop alone; they
had small encouragement from Mother who was the very antithesis
of the classic stage mamma. Any pushing we got from her was
away from the theater not into it; she hated for us to be noticed, even
when an achievement might be worthy; her preference for me, in
particular was that I be nondescript, devoid of opinions, and most
of all that I conform. But just the same, my first appearance on any
stage came about through my poor Mamma. Lost in the loneliness of
Pop's neglect, she had joined a ladies' lodge, the Maccabees, and on
one occasion its members persuaded her to let me sing at an annual
entertainment. But Mother chose my song, which, expressing her
revolt against sex, was in praise of an affection between two girls.
The verse stated that men might be all right in the aggregate, but they
could never provide the satisfaction of (and here comes the title)

> *Just one girl*
> Only just one girl
> There are others I know but
> They're not like Pearl.
> Sun or rain
> She is just the same
> I'll be happy forever
> With just one girl.

Mother managed to drag Pop to the entertainment where he
listened to his child deliver the lyrics in a quavering voice and to the
round of applause from those undemanding Maccabees; at any rate
the episode put it into Pop's mind that I might become a professional.
Not long afterward he telephoned Mother from a saloon near the
Alcazar Theatre and told her to bring me right down; that he had
suggested me for a part in a play called *May Blossom*, and that by
no means was I to let slip the fact that I had never appeared on a
professional stage.

Opposed to the idea as Mother was, she obediently took me to the theater, where I was introduced to its manager, Walter Belasco. He was a half-brother of David Belasco, who was in San Francisco at the time, having come all the way from New York to direct *May Blossom*, of which he was co-author. So I began my acting career under the auspices of the great David Belasco himself.

One engagement I played as a child was the Tivoli Opera House, the home of a permanent company which produced the standard comic operas of that day: *The Mikado, Robin Hood, The Belle of New York*, etc. The star of the company was a handsome, robust comedian, Ferris Hartman, whose son Paul, with his wife Grace, rose to stardom years later in New York. In 1950 they asked me to appear on a radio program called *Breakfast with the Hartmans*, and we recalled fondly our childhood in San Francisco.

My theatrical career was much more active than Gladys's, and the reason must have been that I was Pop's favorite, so he neglected her and pushed me. Gladys couldn't have been a worse actress than I was, and we were equally uninterested in the profession. But the only time I was ever turned down for a job was once when I was sent for to play a part with a road company at the old California Theater. At the first sight of me the leading lady was annoyed by the length of my hair. "The audience will be gasping over that mop of hair," she said, "and it will completely ruin the scene." I actually didn't blame her, for I hated that hair myself and longed to whack it off (which was just what I did in New York several years later and possibly became the first girl ever to be bobbed and windblown).

During our schooldays my mother's main concern was to keep us in respectable neighborhoods. She purposely selected one of our homes because it was across from the Denman Grammar School on Bush Street which was exclusively for girls. In any ordinary city schoolchildren who were also actresses would have been freaks. But San Francisco was anything but ordinary. It was so cosmopolitan that many of our schoolmates were Chinese, French, Spanish and Japanese. I was often hard put in my typically Loos desire to be different. There was an occasion when a reporter for the

Chronicle came to the school to interview students on the subject
of our ambitions. I realized I would never be quoted among so
many others unless I chose a highly original *métier.* Because quite
a number of little girls said they wanted to be actresses, I knew such
an ambition was bound to put my interview into the discard, even
though I already had a head start on that career. I searched my brain
for something that would be newsworthy, a career none of the others
could possibly think of. Finally I hit it: I told the reporter I intended
to become an architect of ocean liners. So it was I who got my
picture taken and made the headline.

During this time there were five other little girls scurrying
around the environs of San Francisco, getting ready to invade the
planet. They were Gertrude Stein, Alice B. Toklas, Elsa Maxwell,
Gertrude Atherton, and Frances Marion, who became rich and
famous writing movie scripts for Mary Pickford, Marie Dressler, and
Wallace Beery. Except for Gertrude Atherton, who remained a San
Franciscan all her life, we all went far afield when young and our
paths crossed only when we were grown up. Frances Marion and
I, being in the movies, met early, and she became my friend, as did
Elsa Maxwell and Alice B. Toklas.

Mother's insistence on a nice home for her children was of
small concern to Pop. Although he was quite "elegant" in a tacky
way, he was such a superb egotist that he was never to learn he
was tacky, and the overwhelming jauntiness of his conceit always
forced one to admire Pop, much as an alcoholic who hates water is
compelled to admire Niagara Falls. In spite of poverty, our family
life was pleasant in the extreme. When Pop did happen to be around
he often used to take us to the French restaurants for which San
Francisco was noted. In all those places the cuisine was of gourmet
quality; a *table d'hôte* dinner used to begin with shrimp or oyster
cocktails made of those small, sweet shrimps or the coppery oysters
which are local specialties. This was followed by petite marmite;
then fish served with some unusual sauce; after which was roast beef,
and, after that, either chicken or game; then came salad, ice cream,
fruit, cheese and coffee. And in the interest of economics let me

state that such a dinner cost twenty-five cents, except in one favorite place, where it was only twenty.

Sometimes when Pop was in an expansive family mood, he used to bring delicacies home in the middle of the night, insisting that we children be hustled out of bed for a treat on which Mother looked with silent disapproval. There were any number of food specialties that were known only to San Francisco. One of them was called an oyster loaf and was made by scooping out a loaf of hard-crusted bread, the inside of which was toasted by some baffling process. The loaf was then stuffed with oysters, which were breaded and fried crisp, but they merged with the toast in a gooey, buttery mass that was delicious.

Another specialty dear to our hearts was the tamale, which had been imported from Mexico; but the chefs of San Francisco improved on the dry, anemic original and turned it into a delectable package of chicken, olives and red peppers wrapped in corn husks lined with Indian meal. There was also chop suey which San Francisco invented *in toto*, and it was so delicious that it was even admired by the Chinese.

Pop's midnight feasts were washed down with lager beer fetched in a bucket from the corner saloon; the bucket, for some reason, was called a "growler", and I loved to go for the beer because the bartender and I were cronies; disloyal to his boss, he taught me to smear the inside of the growler with butter, thus preventing a collar of foam and giving me more beer for my nickel.

There were periods when Pop would be away for several days, hanging out with a colony of bohemian friends who occupied a row of abandoned cable cars parked along the beach. But when he was in residence, we sometimes enjoyed the very fine company of his pals. One of them was a young girl who wrote poetry; I'm sure Pop liked her not so much for her poems as for the fact that she was so extraordinarily pretty. It was a great shock one day to learn that she had killed herself, leaving three lines of poetry which I still remember:

It is a silver space between two rains,
The world is drained of color.
Light remains.

Another frequent guest of ours was a rich Chinese merchant
who overwhelmed us children with presents, as is the custom of that
race. He was typical of the native-born Chinese of San Francisco,
who combine the grace and humor of their race with the alert
knowhow of the New World. Sometimes our friend called on us
wearing an Oriental banker's long coat, for which he apologized,
saying that his old-world business associates looked askance at
Occidental dress

Another of Pop's glamorous friends was Willie Britt, a San
Francisco-born prize fighter, I think a middleweight champion. He
was a charmer and the first matinee idol in the boxing profession. It
was Willie Britt who introduced ladies into the audiences at boxing
matches.

Two brothers who were journalists on San Francisco
newspapers sometimes showed up at our house; they were Wallace
and Will Irwin. Wallace was to become known for his *Love Sonnets
of a Hoodlum* and for humorous stories about a Japanese schoolboy
called Hashimura Togo. Will Irwin's claim to fame was an inspired
book about San Francisco before the fire, *The City That Was.*

Another associate of Pop's, then unknown, was Jack London,
whose masterpiece, *The Call of the Wild,* was yet to be written. Jack
London wasn't sufficiently housebroken to be taken into the presence
of my gentle mother. Pop never brought him home; the time they
spent together was in saloons along the waterfront, where Jack was
soaking up inspiration for *John Barleycorn,* a book he wrote much
later about the horrors of drink. But Jack and Pop had little else in
common, for Jack was an intellectual, one of the first Americans to
read Nietzsche and Schopenhauer, whereas Pop was an egghead only
in a hirsute way.

Pop's acquaintance with Wilson Mizner was sketchy. He was
far below Pop's age group, so I never encountered America's most
fascinating outlaw as a child, but seeing that I was an acceptable

companion for both Pop and Uncle Horace at a tender age, I like to think that a *simpatia* might have developed between us even then. As it turned out, my fondness for Wilson Mizner came many years later. Pop's one recreation in the great outdoors came while he was fishing, a sport in which he loved to indulge on the San Francisco piers. I often used to accompany him, although I was interested not so much in the fish as in the passers-by. The San Francisco waterfront was a wonderfully exciting place, international in character and with a strong flavor of the Orient. Ships from every country in the world poured a stream of roustabouts into the waterfront saloons, which even in 1900 were still engaged in shanghaiing. Just to walk the streets bordering the bay was an exciting adventure, especially when the fog rolled in from the sea. The fog of San Francisco was unlike that of other cities: first of all it was clean, and the brisk scent of salt and seaweed made it an invigorating tonic. When fog veiled San Francisco, everything seemed more than usually mysterious and romantic. One day as Pop and I were fishing off the pier in a heavy mist, a voice of delirious beauty rose from quite close by, singing Mimi's song from *La Boheme*. In our sense of isolation, the song seemed to be for us alone, but at its end an invisible audience broke into applause that echoed near and far from every direction. The unseen singer could only have been Luisa Tetrazzini, who loved San Francisco and sang every year at the Tivoli Opera House.

It was on the San Francisco waterfront that I met an unforgettably seductive creature who was the wife of a captain on a freighter that plied between the California coast and the Orient. She came originally from Vermont, as had my grandma. She had green-blue eyes which made a fascinating contrast to the deep tan of her skin and intensified that peculiarly fierce New England type of sex appeal which, in her case, was still strong although she was weather-beaten and spare and her hair had turned gray. She took a fancy to me and invited me aboard her husband's ship. Her one great interest in life was sex, and day after day, as we sat on deck outside the captain's quarters, she undertook to speak to me of intimacies my poor mother was too embarrassed ever to mention; but her slant on the subject was so extremely poetic that she never quite got down to cases. One day when I went over to see her, determined to ask for some more explicit details, I found the freighter had pulled out and she was off on another high venture with her husband, who in thirty years had never sailed without her. Since bona fide marriages are so uncommon, I record this as one of the few I've ever run across.

My experience with that captain's wife left me with visions of mysterious bliss which might also be dangerous; for she warned me that a girl could love not wisely but too well, in which case a child might be born disgracefully out of wedlock. Her stories made such a powerful impression on me that from time to time feelings of excitement and anticipation mingled with downright fear used to come over me in waves.

If it seems incredible that a youngster raised on the very edge of the Barbary Coast in a wicked city like San Francisco could have been so ignorant of the facts of life, I can only explain that in those days sex was a private matter that was seldom discussed; there was no movie which dared to treat the subject realistically, and no television to cover sex crimes. (This brings to mind a TV interview I recently heard, when a newscaster questioned a child who had just been raped. "And how did you feel, Mildred, after this experience?" asked the interviewer; after which the little girl added her bit to the data on the subject by answering, "I felt awful.")

During all the time that Mother was left out of Pop's affairs she tried to lead her brood into the ordinary pursuits of an average family. When summer arrived she took us to the old ranch in Etna for our vacation, leaving Pop to his citified pleasures. Then, too, there was an extra occasion when we were all called north for Grandma's funeral and she was finally taken away from the room where she had spent most of her life. While on those visits, we were led into all the activities of a big ranch by our four country cousins; we gathered eggs by the hundreds, romped in the hay, and frolicked in the granary until our clothes were full of wheat. But I was always happiest in San Francisco with my Pop, savoring the *simpatia* I felt for him, trying to imitate the way he made everybody laugh.

It's difficult to remember old jokes, but I can cite a not-so-funny one I happened to get off at a time when Gladys and I were

appearing in *Quo Vadis* with the Alcazar Stock Company. We were
cast as Christian children awaiting contact with some lions in an
off-stage arena. Now it so happened that my poor unprofessional
mother had chosen tights for us of a violent yellow hue, and when
we showed up in them at dress rehearsal the director was furious
because, naturally, we were supposed to be bare-legged.(We might
have dispensed with tights altogether, but for even children to have
appeared without them in that era would have been disreputable.)
While the director was loudly criticizing Mother in front of the
whole company, I piped up to suggest that he insert a line of dialogue
saying that owing to the persecutions of the Roman emperor,
we Christian children had contracted jaundice. My flippancy so
embarrassed Mother that she wasn't even grateful that I caused the
director to laugh away his disapproval.

When I was around the age of eight I wrote my first piece for
publication. A children's magazine, *St. Nicholas*, had announced
a contest in which contributions were to take the form of an
advertisement for a floor polish known as F.P.C. Wax. Naturally I
knew nothing about F.P.C. Wax but, with a larceny which might do
credit to Madison Avenue, I wrote an ad in verse, accompanied by
the drawing of a Man from Mars. I can remember that ad even now:

The best thing I've seen, said the Man from Mars
Since I left my abode from among the stars
Is something my own world sadly lacks
The earth's greatest boon F.P.C.Wax.

I won the competition. The prize of five dollars was instantly
borrowed by Pop who made a deal that I was to be paid interest at the
rate of 10 per cent a week. When that 10 per cent finally amounted
to more than the loan, I told Pop to forget about the capital and just
come through with the interest. But I was only kidding; I never
expected to get my money back and would even have felt let down
had Pop returned it. Although unaware, I was beginning to sense
the thrill a girl can feel in handing money to a man. This is a trait
in us that has been put to good account by most of the great lovers
of the world; the Don Juans, who never gave gifts to loved ones that

were in any way commensurate with their means; In fact the reason that mother-love itself is so exhilarating is that it provides so many opportunities for self-sacrifice. The most powerful love stories share the same premise: Cleopatra most certainly supported Marc Antony, and the Queen of Sheba provided Solomon with luxuries which, even as a king, he couldn't afford. Men, too, can wax downright emotional over being kept; poems like the Song of Songs will never be written to a gold-digger.

A day finally arrived in San Francisco when our finances took a sudden upturn. Grandma Smith died, and overnight my mother became an heiress. It was then that Pop really splurged. But on Mother's insistence he first bought us a slick new house in a district near the Presidio on Union Street; after feeling that he had amply provided for his family, Pop proceeded to get rid of the remainder of my mother's inheritance as rapidly as he could. Since he was an expert, it didn't take Pop long; soon everything was lost, and Grandpa was no longer around to fall back on.

At this new low ebb of our fortunes, someone made Pop the offer of a job. It was to manage a theater in Los Angeles, one which featured that exciting new form of entertainment to which the public had just given the affectionate nickname, "the movies." Our pleasant home on Union Street was sold, and we were left with only enough money to provide transportation to Los Angeles for three of us and leave a small fund with Clifford so he might pursue medical studies at Stanford University. So at long last we were through with San Francisco, the lovely, lively, openhearted, amoral city which has lingered in memory as my spiritual home

---

❧ *Robert McNamara*

Memories of peace, nightmares of war

The day after John F. Kennedy's inauguration was among the proudest of my life. At four o'clock that afternoon, January 21, 1961, I gathered with my nine fellow cabinet nominees in the East Room of the White House to be sworn in. We stood in a semicircle beneath the crystal chandelier facing Chief Justice Earl Warren in his black robes. I took my oath of office in unison with the others as President and Mrs. Kennedy, congressional leaders, and our families watched. Then the president stepped forward to congratulate us.

I was now the eighth, and youngest ever, secretary of defense. But even though I was just forty-four, I was not the youngest in the group. The president was forty-three; Robert Kennedy was thirty-five. Like many of these men, I had grown up in the years between the world wars and had served as a young officer in World War II.

President Kennedy knew I would bring to the military techniques of management from the business world, much as my Harvard colleagues and I had done as statistical control officers in the war. I was thrilled to be called again to work for my country.

My road to the East Room had begun in San Francisco. My earliest memory is of a city exploding with joy. It was November 11, 1918—Armistice Day. I was two years old. The city was celebrating not only the end of World War I but the belief, held so strongly by President Woodrow Wilson, that the United States and its allies had won the war to end all wars.

They were wrong, of course. The twentieth century was on its way to becoming the bloodiest, by far, in human history: during it, 160 million people have been killed in wars across the globe.

I was part of a World War I baby boom that caused a classroom shortage by the time I entered first grade in 1922. My class was housed in a wooden shack. The accommodations were poor, but the teacher was superb. At the end of the month she gave us a test and reassigned our seating based on the results; the student with the highest grade would sit in the front seat in the leftmost row.

I was determined to occupy that seat. The class was predominantly WASP—white Anglo-Saxon Protestants—but my competitors for the top spot were invariably Chinese, Japanese, and Jews. After each week of hard work, I would spend Saturday and Sunday playing with my neighborhood friends while my rivals went to ethnic schools, studied their ancestral languages, absorbed ancient and complex cultures, and returned to school on Monday determined to beat their Irish classmate. I am happy to say they rarely did.

My drive for scholastic excellence reflected the fact that neither my mother nor my father had gone to college (my father never went beyond eighth grade), and they were fiercely determined that I would. Their resolve shaped my life.

Each human being looking back on his or her life—in my case, looking back on seventy-eight years—can identify defining events that influenced what they became and why they believed as they did.

One was the Great Depression. I was graduated from high school in 1933, At the time, fully 25 percent of the adult males of this country were unemployed. The father of one of my classmates committed suicide because he could not feed his family. Another friend, the daughter of a wealthy family, joined the Communist Party.

Violent labor strikes were common. During the West Coast maritime strikes of 1934 and 1936, there were machine-gun emplacements on roofs and along the waterfront in San Francisco to prevent fighting on the docks. Once, on Market Street I saw a longshoreman corner a man he thought was a strikebreaker. He knocked the man down, pinned one of his knees on the curb with his ankle on the street, and stamped on the shin to shatter the bones. The violence shocked me.

I learned firsthand about the conditions that were helping to spark the violence when I went down to the Union hiring hall in the summer of 1935 and applied for a job at sea to earn money for my next semester at college. I shipped out as an ordinary seaman on the freighter SS *Peter Kerr*. The pay was twenty dollars a month, there was no running fresh water in the crew's quarters, the bunks were so infested with bedbugs that one morning I counted nineteen bites on one leg, and the food was inedible---I was in superb physical shape, but lost thirteen pounds during the voyage. The experience gave me sympathy for the plight of unorganized labor that still influences me. As an executive in the auto industry, I admired union leaders like Walter Reuther, and at the Pentagon I tried to recruit Jack Conway, a United Auto Workers official, as my assistant secretary for manpower.

Let me be simple and direct. I want to be clearly understood: the United States of America fought in Vietnam for eight years for what it believed to be good and honest reasons. By such action, administrations of both parties sought to protect our security, prevent the spread of totalitarian Communism, and promote individual freedom and political democracy. The Kennedy, Johnson, and Nixon administrations made their decisions and by those decisions demanded sacrifices and, yes, inflicted terrible suffering in light of those goals and values.

Their hindsight was better than their foresight. The adage echoes down the corridors of time, applying to many individuals, in many situations, in many ages. People are human; they are fallible. I concede with painful candor and a heavy heart that the adage applies to me and to my generation of American leadership regarding Vietnam. Although we sought to do the right thing—and believed we were doing the right thing—in my judgment, hindsight proves us wrong. We both overestimated the effect of South Vietnam's loss on the security of the West and failed to adhere to the fundamental principle that, in the final analysis, if the South Vietnamese were to be saved, they had to win the war themselves. Straying from this central truth, we built a progressively more massive effort on an inherently unstable foundation. External military force cannot substitute for the political order and stability that must be forged by a people for themselves.

In the end, we must confront the fate of those Americans who served in Vietnam and never returned. Does the unwisdom of our intervention nullify their effort and their loss? I think not. They did not make the decisions.

They answered their nation's call to service. They went in harm's way on its behalf. And they gave their lives for their country and its ideals. That our effort in Vietnam proved unwise does not make their sacrifice less noble. It endures for all to see. Let us learn from their sacrifice and, by doing so, validate and honor it.

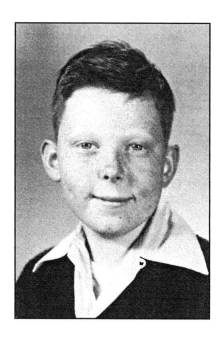

✒ *Robert Carson*

Standing on the waterfront and looking not just out,
but in.

EXILES OF THE CITY

When I was born in San Francisco, there were
long shadows cast still from a General Strike, a World War,
Memories flared on the lit end of cigars.
Always the puff and swollen fires, men's breath,
the city would breathe and choke and hustle
to the rhythms—newspaper hawkers,
the whiz-spin of rollers sending endless
boxes into dark holes in trucks and ships.

Women fresh from the war plants, assembly-line slavery,
cranked out the children—buggies and strollers
left alone in the sun on the pavement,
as if to exile us and teach us early about
the wind and fog and salt, the cool hands of the street.
Soon we fingered, with false bravado,
the handles of knives, roamed in packs,
danced to the tune of mass production:
the factories and ours.

Each birthday party a Nationalist feast:
Italian, French, Irish. Filipino, Indian.
Somehow it all drew together, breathing in all
Something of the gypsy, something of the Arts.
All had their hands on the rollers, gears, switches,
winches of the city.

There were the constant sailings and homecomings.
Maybe, we thought, beyond the ice-man (back-slick apron)
beyond the butcher (blood-stained apron), even beyond the
rollers, warehouses, docks, and the space between
the bridges we could find the world growing out,
opened naturally like spring flowers and trees.
Sailors brought the tales, and we hornpiped them
through the streets. Snaking through the sunlight,
 tasting smells, the salt and bread, excited our blood,
soon we made connections with the bay, black connections,
down so far we compressed, squeezed in a mass,
learned of people who slept under foundations deep in the city,
fish with bigger gills, fire-bomb at the end of the
tokay rainbow, eyes exploded, puffed and floated,
belly up on the beaches.

Nothing remains the same—coming home from work and war
and the sea—knowing the lines of ocean's poem,
or breath in the sail. Distant and longer shadows..
The fog that laces in and out: Coast's continual breathing
ritual with interior valleys.
Some return in airless plastic bags
with name tags to match the death letters
and the neatness of automation processing
bodies wrapped in vinyl.
We raised cargo nets, nets around the city,
teaming with gods and fish and life.
Knife slashing edges, the sting of salt and blood.

Suddenly a loosening, the faintest falling,
simple remembrances: sun and ice, cement and salt
the last heavy-veined leaf from all the branches of thought.
Tremulous journey to earth.
Blowing down past the office buildings,
Black-glass-garbled reflections of ships and bay and fog,
life we never knew.

We return to the tolling of bells,
buoyed in every night,
church bells, buoy bells, ships' bells.
Narrowing lanes from sea to the city.
Sliding between missing sounds of dreams we never built.
The leaf scratching down the streets,
Whirling the tones of our own exile.

RETAKE THE CITY

Why do these dreams recur-
The tender, the brutal-
Never allowing a separation
To savor or scorn just one.

Dreams of light, sleight of hand,
Elongation of a raindrop
freefalling
reaching out to splatter
on cement and steel.

The last heavy-veined leaf
from all the branches of thought-
A work partner pummeled to eternity
head first in a glorious swandive.
Slipping on a containership,
 the steel and cement closing down…

Dull thud we all pretended
not to hear.

A clerk, clipboard in hand,
squashed against a 20 ton container
scattered over a retaining wall.
Don't slip on his liver.

Flowing days
of all our futures.
We set to work
Knowing the water, fog, light,
cement and salt.

These are dreams
and these are realities

into which we all
have fallen
and daily return
suspended like bridges
over the final bay of the world.

Bells toll,
Crossing Dolores Park,
Portsmouth Square, Washington Square.
Whirling tones-
Bells, Colors-
Tones of work partners
Spiraling through space.

City of generations
Who all have fallen
in dreams' gentle violence.
The leaf separated from the tree
falling over the edge of memory.

Bells for forgotten men.
Wanderers, Workers, Poets.
Returning home
The tones of dusk in watercolor.
The sun mixing with the sea.

Bells that toll for survival:
Everyday you must remake,
Everyday you must reshape,
Everyday you must retake
The City.

✒ *Carol Channing*

Discovering the cathedral, embracing the faith

Before I ever attended any live theatre or concert or opera, my mother asked me if I'd like to volunteer to deliver *Christian Science Monitors* on Saturdays to the back stages of all the then legitimate theaters in San Francisco, where we lived. I was told I was a cooperative and tractable child, so I agreed in order to live up to being cooperative and tractable.

We went first to the Curran Theatre, but not to the lobby or the box office, no. We walked down that long, dark alley leading to the Curran's huge stage door, which is still there. I must have been small, because the iron bolt that's so easy for me to slide open today when we play San Francisco was nearly impossible for me to budge at that time. The door was a clean, newly painted gray. I remember I decided the paint must be sticking it closed, so I put down my

Monitors to tackle it. My mother opened the heavy door quite easily. I stepped inside and stood still. I was overcome with the feeling that here was hallowed ground. I couldn't move. I could see the stage even in the dark, through what I now know to be "3." (Stages are usually divided into five sections.) It came over me that I was looking at the stage and backstage of a cathedral, a temple, a mosque, a mother church. I know I'm using adult words to describe a child's feelings, but I don't know how else to tell you this simple reaction of a child to a holy place. Children know it. They sense it's holy.

I put the publications in the rack by the door and have no idea how long I stood there. I remember my mother seemed to have someplace else to go, because I was alone and still in awe and unrushed. Beyond that stage door, when we finally got it open, lay the real life…the only real life there is, not just the mundane facts of life, the mathematical statistics, but a world created by human beings who have caught a glimpse of creation and then re-created their glimpse to put it inside that door and onto the stage. I didn't want to leave.

When Mother returned to me she said, "Now we'll go next door to the Geary Theater and then to the old Tivoli Opera House," where I later saw Leo Carrillo in some play about a pushcart vendor selling garlic and onions, played to an audience howling with laughter. And then on to the President Theatre, where Charlotte Greenwood played with Joe E. Brown in *Elmer the Great*… hilarious…and Henry Duffy and Dale Winter presented *Sally, Irene, and Mary*…beautiful ! Of course, at that moment I hadn't seen any live shows yet. At that time, I wanted only to kiss the floorboards of these religious monuments. But how did I know then they were really churches? Children sense things, don't they?

My first taste of life in front of a live audience came when I was in the fourth grade, while I was sitting in the audience of the auditorium of the Commodore Sloat grammar school (first to sixth grades) in St. Francis Wood (one of the residential sections of San Francisco). The occasion was the school assembly meeting, which took place on Fridays. This meeting was for the purpose of nominating the next term's school officers. An electric shock went through me when Bobbie Schmaltz nominated me for secretary of the student body. If you were nominated, the procedure was to walk forward to the stage, go up the six steps to center stage, and tell your fellow students why they should vote for you. I was ossified with fright on the walk up because naturally I couldn't think of one reason why they should vote for me. I got as far as when I was supposed to speak.

I was an only child, and like so many only children I had nightly imaginary visits with anyone I met that I thought was eccentric or funny or adorable or had an accent different from mine. During these "visits," I spread out teacups over the assembled chairs and carried on conversations with all of these fascinating people. Guests would often ask my parents, "Who are all of those people upstairs with Carol?" My mother would reply, "No, that's only Carol. She's playing by herself." "No," the skeptical guests would say, "who are all of those voices?"

So, in the morning assembly, in the school auditorium, with my knees shaking, I did the thing I did best…turned into somebody else. I did an imitation of the principal of the school, Miss Berard, saying, "When you fill out your ballots, vote for Carol." My classmates yelled their recognition of Miss Berard, applauded, and everyone laughed, including Miss Berard. Even she enjoyed it! My knees were steadier now.

In the middle of the stage, suddenly I was no longer an only child. What I laughed at alone in my room, everyone else laughed at. I suddenly realized we're all alike. What I was excited with, everyone else seemed to be excited with. We all go toward the same things or away from them. We laugh or cry at the same things. We're safe and close together under one roof, experiencing reactions simultaneously. Nothing else in the world matters. Only this delicious moment. We don't care what's wrong with any of us, we're free! We were soaring above all the faults we are supposed to have. And at that moment, all of our happiness quotients were soaring, including mine. To the sound of applause, I ran off the stage, into the cloakroom, hid behind the coats, and cried, "O, God, I'll do anything to get back on that stage again. I'll go without food, water, sleep, or anything."

That night I told my parents, "Something happened to me today. I can't stop thinking of it." They listened. I told them all about it. My father, after focusing intently on what I said, announced, "There's an adage that says, "Be careful what you set your heart upon for you shall surely get it."

Me: You mean I can lay down my life right now?

Daddy: You can lay down your life at seven or at seventy-seven or whatever. The happier people are not the ones who get *out* of work. The happier people are the ones who are lucky enough to *find* their work. I noticed he said happ*ier*. None of us is completely happy, because challenges seem to be a constant in our lives. Maybe sometime we'll find out why.

At school we were given until the next Friday to get our campaign speeches together. First I rehearsed mine on my mother, who was always there when I got home from school. Then I tried it on my father an hour before dinner, when he got home from the office, and then on any of their dinner guests, who were not the best comedy audience in the world since they usually had an incurable problem or two or they wouldn't have been Christian Scientists. But I soon found out, after I won the election (Naturally I won, because my campaign speech created holy chaos). I found out that the fewer rehearsal laughs there were from my parents' friends, the better the final performance for my fellow students went.

The best part of running for secretary was that the auditorium held only one-third of the student body, so we had to do three assembly meetings. On the first one I wasn't so good. The second I was better. By the third I was swinging, and that's when I learned to like long runs.

My adolescent years were spent in Aptos Junior High (now called Middle School). Joy! I had an entire new battery of faculty members and students to take home with me in my imagination. However, in this school, parliamentary procedure took place only in each individual class of about thirty. The president and vice

president functioned with, and were elected by, the entire school.
So, naturally, I ran this time for vice president of the entire student
body. I gravitated to the school band because I needed them for my
campaign song.

The leader of the school band was Harry Kullijian. I was so in
love with Harry I couldn't stop hugging him. In hindsight, I realize
how disciplined he was and what a sense of responsibility he had.

Remember, these were times way before the Pill. Now
condoms are necessary, we hear, but the Pill, I'm sure we all agree,
caused the sexual revolution. It wasn't so bad using discipline
instead. I was free to adore Harry, to sink into his protection and
dearness. It was thrilling and sweet to have his arms around me.
Anyway, I was eleven and Harry was fifteen, a little older than most
in our class because his Armenian family didn't believe in starting
children in school until later. I know how right they were, because
I started kindergarten early for those days, four and a half years old,
and skipped second grade, so I was younger than everybody all our
growing up years. I still feel most of the world is smarter than I
am. It may be, but it leaves one with a weird lack of conviction in
comparison with the positive statements other people seem to make.
My son, Channing, also graduated high school at sixteen. He seems
to be all right, though.

Harry confided to my mother how affectionate I was to him.
By this time we were twelve and sixteen. He had a serious talk with
both my parents (without me) assuring them, "I will never get your
Carol into any kind of trouble." They told me about the talk.

My father said, "I like that boy."

Naturally, it was the most difficult thing in the world not to
make love to Harry, not that I knew anything about how to make
love, or what it was leading to. I just wanted to be close to him
and hug him from head to toe. But he would distract me, and we'd
rush to the beach to see (for twenty-five cents, through a periscope
pointing downward) how the man buried alive was doing or run to
Golden Gate Park, where Joe DiMaggio was training every Saturday
and Sunday.

How did we know that Joe was great even then? I told about growing up at the same time as Joe on a TV interview in New York. We all worshipped Joe. Decades later, I was one of hundreds on a big TV special called *Night of 100 Stars*. The entire cast was assembled for a picture. A voice called from behind me, "We miss you out at the ballpark, Carol."

I turned around and, yes…you knew: it was Joe! With that smile you could only describe as sunny Italy. You died only a few years ago, Joe, but I wish I could correct you. It wasn't the ballpark. It was where Eighth Avenue enters Golden Gate Park in San Francisco. There was a big clearing there with nothing but grass. You had only one or two other players to throw you your ball. I always wanted to straighten you out about that, but I never had the nerve to go and talk with you, even at the time I was starring in *Gentlemen Prefer Blondes*. You didn't have a ballpark to practice in then. You never stopped concentrating long enough to look up and see the same group of schoolchildren watching you every Saturday and Sunday with no one else there. I think nobody knew you were you then, except us, and we surely knew…years ahead of time..

My ballet mistresses were Madame Hirsch and Mademoiselle Arnold. I was thirteen years old when they submitted my name to Adolph Bolm, the choreographer and master of the San Francisco Opera Ballet. He accepted me! My first appearance was in the ballet *Petrouchka*—on pointe. The second was with Elizabeth Rethberg singing something by Wagner. Third, the Russian Ballet. All bit parts. I dressed with all of the Russian ballerinas, but time stood still when Tatiana Riabouchinska asked me, in Russian, to hook her tutu up the back. I knew what she was asking me to do because it wasn't hooked. I had watched her dance for years, every time she came to San Francisco, and never thought I'd meet her..

Where else could this happen? I took lessons from Yeichi Nimura, Japan's greatest dancer, and learned his "Saw Dance" (Sword Dance). Then I studied with La Argentina, Spain's world-renowned flamenco dancer. I saved my allowance for fifty-cent seats in the top balcony of the Curran or Geary Theatre and saw

Kreutzberrg and Giorgi, Mary Wigman, Trudi Schoop (dance pantomimist) from Berlin, Angna Enters from Paris, and Uday Shan Kar from India. I can still do his neck wiggle, but you had to have started doing it when you were little.

San Francisco is a deliciously enchanting city!

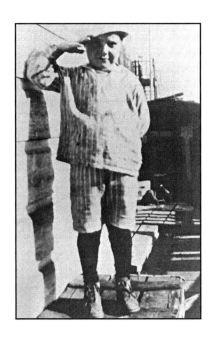

✒ *Joe DiMaggio*
By Richard Ben Cramer

Learning to hit, smoke and play cards at North Beach Playground.

Joe Di Maggio sat on the tar of the playground with his back against the wall on the Powell Street side, his legs cocked in front of him like a couple of pickets. At fifteen, Joe was mostly legs—leg-bones more like it—and a head taller than his friends. It was Niggy Fo who gave him his nickname, Coscilunghi—that meant "Long-legs" in Sicilian.

All the boys on the North Beach playground had names—that meant you were in, you belonged there. There was Shabby Minafo and his brother Bat (he only wanted to bat), and Hungry Geraldi (he could really eat); Friggles Tomei had those fancy feet at second base; Lodigiani they called Dempsey, because he once decked a guy in a fight; and Niggy, of course, got his name for his dark skin. They were always on the playground or on the street. Who had room at home? On this spring afternoon, in 1930, they were playing Piggy on a Bounce—one guy with a bat, everyone else in the field, and one guy would hit till someone caught the ball, or caught it on one bounce, and then the batter had to take the field.

Joe was at the playground most days, too…but like today—not exactly with them. He'd come out of his house, down the hill from Taylor Street—but he'd sit apart, watching in silence, arms draped across his knees in a pose of solitary sufficiency. Or maybe it wasn't all pose. Joe was different from the other guys. They always wanted to play ball. They were desperate to play ball—even if they could barely play. Joe could play. But you had to get him to play.

Bat Minafo and Frank Venezia always picked the teams. They were little guys, but pretty good players. They'd flip a coin, and whoever won would pick Joe. Guys would actually say, "Oh, you got Joe, you're gonna win." It wasn't just the way Joe could hit. (Even those mushy city-issue softballs, Joe could hammer them the length of the playground, a block and a half, into the swimming pool.)…But more than that, it was the way he was in a game. He had to win. That was the reason he'd play—he wanted to win something. Sometimes, Bat and Frank would make everybody throw in a nickel or a dime, and they'd play winner-take-all. Then Joe would play, for sure. But playing just to play…well, mostly, he'd sit.

In the long fingers of his right hand, he'd dangle a smoke in front of his shins—if no one was looking. There were rules about smoking, but not for Joe. The playground assistant was a guy named Rizzo. He only had one arm, but he played a mean game of tennis. He'd throw the ball up, whip his racket around with the same hand, and *bang*—the guy could murder the ball. No one but Joe could return his serve. So Rizzo let Joe smoke—sort of a tip of the cap.

Still, Joe was furtive, so no one would mooch. If he had a pack, he'd keep it in his sock. If anybody saw it, that pack was a goner. Mostly he'd roll his own. A pouch of Bull Durham cost the same five cents, but he could roll a hundred smokes. A nickel was something to hold on to in Joe's world.

At that Powell Street playground wall, he was at the center of everything he knew. There, arrayed in front of him, chasing that city softball. Laughing at each other, tearing their shoes on the tar, were the boys who were personages in his life—apart from his family, it was almost everybody who mattered.

They all lived within ten tight blocks. Joe knew their little brothers, who tagged along and tried to play. He knew their sisters, who played rotation basketball at the hoop past left center field . (Well, he knew the sisters by sight: Joe never said five words in a row to anybody's sister.) He knew all their houses, and who slept where. He knew their mothers, and where they shopped. He knew what their fathers fished.

On the left, past third base, was the boys' bathroom. Joe spent a lot of time in there, playing cards. Joe was good at cards. But that was like baseball: he wasn't just playing. Joe and Niggy Marino used to box the cards—fix the deck—or they'd play partners, and kick each other to signal for discards: five kicks meant to throw the five, two for the deuce, etc. By the time they finished, their legs were black-and-blue. But they went home with a few extra nickels— money from the patsies. Poor Frank Venezia! He played all the time and never caught on they were cheating him. But that was Frank. He just thought he was lousy at cards.

Past the outfield, past the basketball and tennis courts and the open swimming pool, Columbus Avenue cut the playground off at an angle. Nothing was exactly square in North Beach—a neighborhood of odd intersections and acute hillside corners—because Columbus sliced through the street grid diagonally from the office buildings downtown, north and west to Fisherman's Wharf. Columbus was the hub for Italian San Francisco, and the boys' windows on the ways of the world. On Columbus, at the corner of the playground, they'd catch the F-car downtown—Stockton Street, all the way to Market. After school, kids rode two for a nickel.

A block and a half up Columbus lay the expanse of Washington Square, the *gran piazza*, like a carpet of green spread in front of the great Sts. Peter and Paul's Church. The Italian Cathedral of the West was at that time only five years old—Joe had seen the whole thing

built. But its massive twin spires, the solemn gleam of the grand
marble altar, even the bright modern classrooms for the School of
Americanization , were designed to bear witness eternally to proud
Italianita and the achievement of his parents' generation. On the
grass in front of the church, the men of the community gathered
every afternoon for coffee (maybe a little wine) and argument—
though Joe's dad seldom made an appearance. Giuseppe DiMaggio
wasn't much for talk.

Near the church on Columbus stood the other institutions of
the grown-up world: there was the Valente-Martini Funeral Home
(you could pass from your christening at Sts. Peter and Paul to a
coffin—hopefully not too fast, but all within a couple of blocks.) Up
the street, there was the community hall, Casa Fugazi, named for
Commendatore John F. Fugazi, a banker and one of the early Italian-
American *prominenti*. At Columbus and Stockton stood the Bank
of America, whose founder, A.P. Gianinni, was most prominent of
all *prominenti*. On Columbus, too, there was the library—but no
one Joe knew went to the library. The boys were more interested in
other cultural sites on Columbus, like LaRocca's Corner, where the
wiseguys played cards all day over cups of LaRocca's homemade
wine. (Prohibition was an approximate science in North Beach, and
Vince LaRocca, Ciccio's uncle, was "well connected".) And nearby
were the nightclubs, the Lido Café and Bimbo's 365 Club, with their
showgirls—tall gorgeous girls, who'd come from all over...though
not from North Beach. No Italian family had showgirls.

From Columbus came food for the neighborhood tables—from
Molinari's big new deli, and Caligari's bakery on Green, just off the
Avenue. On Columbus at Green was the Buon Gusto Market, and off
Columbus, on Powell, there was Celli's, where they made the best
pasta and let you buy on credit. In Joe's crowd, there were months
when everybody ate on credit—say, before crab season began.
Clothes, same way: without credit, you'd wear your big brothers'
stuff forever. Every family ran a tab at Tragone's, on Columbus, for
clothes and shoes. You could get the shoes cheaper at Gallenkamp's
on Kearny street—but that was all the way downtown. (And it was
some kind of Kraut chain, strictly cash-and-carry.)

Three blocks west of the playground was Joe's first school, Hancock Elementary, just up the alley from his house. The school was built into a downslope, so the recess yard in front of the school was a flat pad of concrete below street level. And a pathway, like a little bridge, led from the street to the school's main door. In that recess yard, the boys used to play a kind of baseball—but with no bat: you'd just whack the ball with your hand and run like hell to first base, which was a basement doorway. Joe was the only boy who could smack the ball over the bridge. He had long arms and big hands he could swing like a hammer. That was his main distinction at Hancock. That and penmanship. One of the teachers, Mrs. Lieboldt, made her kids do every exercise in the workbook— perfect round O's, straight lines crossing T's…then she gave out fancy certificates: "For acquired excellence in practical BUSINESS WRITING by study and practice from the Zaner Method of Arm Movement Writing. (The Zaner-Bloser Co., Columbus, Ohio)." It was the only school honor Joe ever won. (But everybody got one, even Niggy Marino—and Niggy got thrown out of all his schools. Even the Ethan Allen School for tough kids, they threw him out.

Joe's second school, two blocks east, was Francisco Junior High. Nobody made him do anything there. Joe and Frank Venezia used to sit in class like a couple of dummies—they never kept up on the reading. The other kids gave all the answers. They just seemed smarter. Actually, Joe wasn't stupid. But he never wanted to open has mouth, say something wrong, and look stupid. That came from home. In the flat on Taylor Street, they talked Sicilian. Everybody laughed at Joe's lousy Sicilian. (Even his little brother, Dommie, made fun of him.) And shame was what Joe couldn't stand. He was a blusher. (That embarrassed him, too.) So, he just grew silent. His sisters talked about him behind his back: they thought he was "slow"…Anyway, Joe didn't have to talk at school. None of the teachers made him talk. They just moved him on, year after year. It was like no one even knew he was there.

In Joe's world, the papas still woke in the middle of the night and walked down the hill to the wharf and their boats. They'd be back in the afternoon, each with a catch to sell, with nets to fold, with maybe a secret paper sack (illegal striped bass, to carry home for supper). In Joe's world, meat was still for Sundays—and Mondays, when the mamma made the leftover scraps into stew or soup.

Maybe Joe's house was poorer than most: nine kids, and a dad whose boat wasn't big enough for crabbing. But everybody had leftovers on Monday---and the same pasta underneath. All the boys on that ballfield could trace their personal histories back to the rocky Sicilian coast—to Sciacca, Porticello, Isola delle Femmine—all the parents came from the same poor towns. Even in the present, on this vast new continent, the lives they made (and taught to their sons) had the clammy jumbled intimacy of the village. Take LaRocca's Corner, up on Columbus: the building was owned by an uncle of the pitcher, Ciccio LaRocca. But the apartment upstairs was the home of the batter, Frank Venezia (Vince LaRocca was his uncle, too). And now that Frank's dad had died (eating bad clams), Vince LaRocca was trying to marry Frank's mamma. This was a world folded in on itself.

And the future…well, that seemed just as contained—and alarmingly close. With Frank's dad dead, Frank would have to go to work, for good. Niggy Marino's dad was sick: Niggy would have to take over the boat. Joe's older brothers Tom and Mike—they already had to go fishing. No one ever saw them playing ball anymore.

Joe didn't want any part of a boat. He couldn't stand the sea, the smell of the fish. But even so, he would have bet five to one his future lay somewhere between that wall on Powell Street and the foot of Columbus—Fisherman's Wharf. At that point, he couldn't see how he would ever escape his father's life, much less the world of North Beach. He barely left the neighborhood now. Why would he? Except when his mamma sent him off to buy meat—that was cheaper over the hill, a half-mile away, in Chinatown. And afternoons he made the trip downtown to sell newspapers. That's how he brought money home—and escaped having to help his dad unload and fold the nets on Fisherman's Wharf.

That's why he was waiting at the playground, that afternoon. He and Frank Venezia would always share a nickel tram fare down to Market Street, to pick up their papers. They should have been on their way already. Joe never liked to wait. And if you showed up late, you could get screwed. They'd give half your papers to some other guy.

"Frank! Come on!" he yelled. "Are you comin' or not?"

But Frank was still batting—Piggy on a Bounce. And he told Joe to cool his heels. Just a few minutes more…he was on a streak!

Joe sold *The Call* at Sutter and Sansome, near the Market Street trolleys. It was three cents for the paper and the kid who sold it got to keep a penny. On a good day, you'd come home with a buck and a half—two bucks or more if the World Series was on or Lindbergh was flying. When Dempsey knocked out Firpo, you could sell 'em for a quarter—people wanted the paper that bad. All the North Beach Boys sold papers, if they didn't have some other job. Tony Santora worked at Hyde and Union, Shabby Minafo had the Standard Oil Building, Dario Lodigiani sold at Montgomery and Sutter, Frank Venezia was three blocks away at Battery and California. Joe had a good corner, banks on both sides and offices stacked on the floors above. By four p.m. there was a steady stream of businessmen heading home. They wanted papers. He didn't have to say a word. Joe's little brother, Dom, started hawking papers before he was ten (he took the corner right across from Joe)—and even Dominic brought home more than a dollar a day.

The best spot was the safety zone where the Market Street trolleys stopped. That was Niggy's. Who was gonna fight him for it? In the safety zone, a guy would flip you a nickel, you'd hand him his paper and then dig around your pockets, like you had to hunt around for two pennies change. Half the time the guy's streetcar would come, and he'd say, "Forget it," and jump on his tram. Niggy was in tight with the wholesaler, Howie Holmes. One day, Howie told Niggy that some guy was giving his paperboys a hard time. So Niggy went and punched the guy out. After that, Howie would leave Niggy's papers in the safety zone. Nig could pick 'em up any time he wanted. Niggy made a lot of friends with his fists.

One afternoon, Niggy's little brother jumped on a streetcar to sell his last papers, but the conductor smacked him, and shooed him off the car. Joe got the number of the tram and told Niggy. The next time that car came through, Niggy jumped on, walked up to the conductor and hit him in the jaw with a straight right hand. The conductor went down—change was rolling all over the car—and Joe and Niggy took off, laughing. Joe still had papers to sell, but, for once, he didn't mind. "You hit him a pretty good shot," he said. Niggy nodded happily: "He won't hit no little kids anymore."

If Joe ever got in a beef, Niggy was there to take care of business. Not that it happened much: Joe never courted trouble with his mouth. And he wasn't the kind to push his way into someone else's fight. That was one thing the guys liked about Joe: he didn't try to be like anybody else. He didn't have to fight. That was fine for Nig. He didn't have to try to talk to girls. That was Ciccio's specialty. Joe was sufficient to Joe.

That's what Frank Venezia admired, why he liked to hang around with Joe. They were both quiet. But Joe was without need to talk. Joe was quiet at the bottom of himself. He had control. That's the way he was with a bat. Never eager, never jumping at the ball. He'd just stand there, while it came to him. Then he'd hit the tar out of it. That was the way he was about everything. If they had a good day selling papers—they had enough to give to their mammas, and then some—Frank would stop with the other guys at the U.S. Restaurant, on Columbus: fried ham on French bread, a big sandwich for a dime. But it wasn't really about the food. They were young, out at night, with money in their pockets—how could they just go home?...But Joe would say, "You guys go on." And he'd be gone, with his dime still in his pocket. Joe always brought his paper money home. His parents were strict about that. But he always had some quarters, if he needed them. For cards. One time, Frank and Joe signed up for the Christmas Club at Bank of America. You'd put in fifty cents a week, and in December, you got a fortune—twenty-five dollars. Frank gave up by summertime, took his money out, blew it that day on a new glove. But Joe kept going and got all the money. And that was his. Frank always figured that Joe's family didn't know about that twenty-five. The way Frank saw it, Joe was always a winner. And in his own eyes, Frank was always a loser.

Except today, with that bat in his hands at Piggy on a Bounce. Frank hit for, musta been, forty-five minutes straight! It was like magic, like he could hit any pitch, any way, anywhere he chose. He could see the ball just sittin' there for him—then he'd cream it. It was like he imagined Joe always felt…*Jesus—Joe!*

Frank had forgotten about Joe sitting there. Frank turned around now. But Joe was gone.

That was the year they'd gotten so close. Frank and Joe had always been friends, but since that past September, they'd spent just about every day together. What happened was, they got to Galileo High School, and that's where their string ran out.

They were hopeless from the day they walked in the door. They'd sit in class, and it was like the rest of the kids had grown up in some other country. "Who knows this?" the teacher would say, and everybody else would stand up, waving their hands with the answer. Joe would look at Frank, Frank would look back at Joe: *What the hell's going on here?*

They'd never taken a book home. But they'd always got through with passing grades—they made no trouble. The only thing they cared about was sports. But at Galileo, they didn't even get into gym class: they got into ROTC, the Army class! As if Joe was gonna march around with a stick on his shoulder, like a *stronzo*. Forget it!

And then, Italian class! The teacher was Mr. Zuberti, a stuck-up Florentine or a Genoese—from up North somewhere, where they thought Sicilians were scum. He'd pick 'em out. Conjugate this verb! (*What the hell's a verb?*)

One morning, Zuberti threw Joe out of class. Joe didn't say a word. Just stood at his desk and walked out, while everybody stared at him. His face was burning red. Joe heard the giggles behind him, as Zuberti sang a little song, in Italian, to Frank: "*Oh, you'll be the next to go…*"

And that was the end. Later that day, in Mrs. Cullen's English class, Joe was sitting next to Tony Santora, and he muttered: "I won't be here this afternoon."

"Why not, Joe?"

"My father comes in with the boat about one. If I don't help clean up, I don't eat tonight."

Of course, that was bullshit. Joe missed most days at Fisherman's Wharf. But this much was true: he didn't come back to school—that day, the next day, or any day thereafter. Frank started playing hooky, too.

They had the same routine. They'd get up in the morning, get ready for school. They'd have some bread, milk with a little coffee, walk out the door and turn down the sidewalk toward Galileo High... then they'd wander off to the park.

They'd hang around Marina Park all morning, watching the older guys with their "tops"—a monte game, where the aces and deuces show up, and you bet against the come. The older guys were always trying to take some young sucker for a buck or two. Joe and Frank would take lunch along, or figure out some way to eat. They could never go near the Wharf: someone would see. The playground was out: they'd be spotted for sure. Sometimes, they'd spend a nickel for the ferry and ride all the way across the Bay—mostly in silence. They were just killing time, like a lot of guys. In that winter, the turn of the 1930s, a couple of young men with time on their hands was nothing to draw a stare. One day, outside the Simmons Bedding plant at Bay and Powell, Frank counted fifty men on the corner. Nobody had anywhere to go. About three o'clock, Joe would have to check in at home. That was the rule in his family, and Joe obeyed rules. He'd bang the door like he was coming home from school, say hello, make sure no one knew anything. Frank had no one to check in with at home. He'd go to the playground, to see if he could get into a game for a while, before they had to go sell papers.

It went on for months—Joe and Frank hanging out all day—until Joe got caught: the school sent a letter home. Joe got a beating from his older brothers. And he was summoned to see the principal, Major Nourse. (No one knew why he was called Major, but the title fit him: he was discipline, first, last, and always.) Tom, the eldest DiMaggio brother, took Joe back to school. But when they got there, Major Nourse wasn't in.

They sat on chairs in the hallway. And they sat.

They sat an hour, an hour and a half. The chairs were hard. They sat.

Finally, Joe said, "Tom. They don't want me."

"Okay," Tom said. They got up and walked out. And that was the last day Joe went to high school.

He promised Tom he'd go to "continuation class"—the school for dropouts. But Joe never went there either.

For a while, he hung around with Frank—who was still on the loose—the school never cared if he came back. But soon, Frank had to go to work. He hooked on—as much as he could—at Simmons Bedding, in the steel mill plant. He tied bed rails into bundles and loaded them onto trucks. That was five bucks a day.

Joe tried his hand as a workin' stiff, too. He worked a week or so for Pacific Box, stacking wooden crates, or bringing slats to the men at the nailing machines. The work was stupid, and the money wasn't great—ten, twelve bucks a week. Joe moved on to the orange juice plant. But that was worse: up to your ass all day in sticky juice, with acid eating into the cuts on your hands. And for what? He didn't even make a full week there.

There wasn't anything that he wanted to do, except to have a few bucks in his pocket—and avoid his father's boat. He went back to selling papers.

Frank thought maybe Joe could hook on at Simmons Bed. They had jobs there if you knew someone. And they had a ball team. Maybe they could both play. He would have talked to Joe about it.

But they weren't talking.

After Frank made Joe wait for Piggy on a Bounce, Joe had to take the streetcar downtown—on his own nickel. After that, Joe wouldn't talk to Frank for a year.

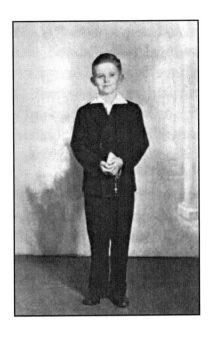

❧ *Kevin J. Mullen*

Listening for the calling, even if it's not the right one.

  In early December 1940 I had been ill and I was allowed to sleep at night in bed with my mother. She then became ill herself and I was removed to the living room couch. On the evening of December 2, my sisters Nancy and Maureen and my infant sister Sheila, who had been born the previous April, were in the kitchen. It was dinnertime and I was still on the living room couch, recuperating from whatever ailed me. My mother called my sister Maureen from the bedroom adjoining the kitchen, and as my sister entered the room, our mother died. According to Maureen at the time, our mother's face was blue. I have since wondered whether I might have been the carrier of the bug that pushed her over the line. I had recently started kindergarten at Kate Kennedy School and been among other young children, excellent transmitters of disease as any teacher will attest. I never did see our mother again; we children were not allowed to attend the funeral. "Windy" Gallagher, I'm told, tried to hustle the church for a free burial gown, claiming that our mother was a member of the Third Order of St. Francis.

My father never slept in the 30th Street house after the night of our mother's death. He was superstitious about death. Certainly there were home-based deaths in his native Ireland and I have never heard of anyone there abandoning their homes on that account. (Frank McCourt's mother, however, did move at least twice to get away from the ghosts of her recently dead children.) Whatever the reason, my father sold the house and its contents, lock stock and barrel. Included in the sale were my mother's photo albums which would have contained any family pictures from earlier San Francisco generations. The mention of the loss of those pictures can still get a rise out of my sisters who credit my father with a lack of sensitivity. In truth, he was a product of his time and place, just as you and I are of ours.

In the days before supermarkets, corner groceries could not keep fresh vegetables and dairy products because of the loss through spoilage. This gave rise to the home delivery businesses and the presence in the city's neighborhoods of trucks filled with vegetables; butter and eggs; fish; and other perishable goods, to be sold directly to housewives at their door. The last vestige of this industry was the milk delivery man who has now passed for the most part into history.

I still run into San Franciscans of a certain age who remember as children the arrival of my father, the "egg man", in their neighborhoods. In those quieter days his arrival constituted an event, at least from a child's perspective. He did pretty well on his route. He later told me that he made enough before the war to pay double house payments on the mortgage on our house.

He served another function in the Irish community as well. In those days, before the widespread proliferation of automobiles, people were pretty much restricted to their own neighborhoods. He moved among the districts as sort of a mobile news agency, learning of the latest local news which he transmitted to his Irish housewife customers elsewhere. For this he was paid with more news or, sometimes, his customers would ply him with a drink to prime the news pump, and to distract him from their mounting unpaid balances.

He reveled in this activity though it often slowed him down on his job. One day I sat waiting in the car for him to make a delivery. I must have been four or five at the time and to my mind he had been gone for too long. To punish him, I removed the pages of the small binder in which he kept his accounts and threw them out the car's window. When he returned he had to round up the pages which by then had been dispersed by the wind. He was angry with me, and I remember that my behavior was a subject of discussion when I got home. But he didn't hit me. It seems I was the only violent one in the family.

When the war came, and gasoline was rationed, he had to suspend operations for the duration. He went to work first as a bus driver and later as a warehouseman at the Marine Building at 100 Harrison Street. He resumed his route after the war and held on for a few years, but the growth of supermarkets—which by now were able to refrigerate perishable foods—finally ended his business. That and unsustainable accounts receivable and the changing social climate in the city.

As a child I was embarrassed in front of my friends by his different accent, working-man's attire, and old fashioned country ways. A product of his time and place, he did not dispense physical affection easily but, unlike many others, he always saw to our creature needs. Even after his little business failed and he took work as a janitor at the age of 49, you could be sure that after a week on the job, the boss would turn over the keys to him. He was highly responsible.

Rose Smith was a widow with five children of her own, and she began "to take in kids," at first on her own and then through Catholic Social Services. First were the Logans, whose mother had died and whose father couldn't care for them. We were next in 1941.

To a kid, World War Two was fun, if that's the word. In the early days, we huddled in the darkness behind drawn shades during air raid drills, straining to hear the sound of enemy planes. Once, a man was shot dead on the Golden Gate Bridge for failing to turn out his headlights during a blackout. We heard he had been signaling enemy subs. One thing I remember about those years was getting in many childish fights. They were harmless enough affairs but suggest to me now that I had a lot of anger in me.

Another impression which remains is that I was always embarrassed about my status at school. We would all get new dark blue uniform corduroy pants at the beginning of the school year. The other kids would get replacements during the year as theirs wore out. Not me, nor anyone else in Mrs. Smith's ménage, I imagine. By years' end, while everyone else still had nice blue cords, mine were faded to grey and patched. That was a blow to my pride which I had in full measure.

I was ashamed to live in what amounted to a foster home. Whether by house dictate or personal shame (probably the former) I knew that I could not bring friends to the house. Once, Rose Smith took the whole passel of us to the circus with complimentary tickets which originated I know not where. She was trying to do for us, I'm sure, but I was humiliated when she asked an usher in our hearing if there was a section set aside for "underprivileged children." I hated being pitied.

Not all was so grim. We had all the neighborhood distractions available to kids at the time. We would play one-foot-off-the-gutter on the "level" (Castro between 22nd and Alvarado). Then there was the double lot above 3919 that ran through to Alvarado where we would play pinky-on-a-bounce or have sod fights when the new weeds sprouted up in the spring. We had a neighborhood dog, Frisco, a mottled grey hound, which actually belonged to George Augustus and which to our mind was the toughest dog in town. I envied the Augustus boys. George would be allowed to go to school on rainy days sans raincoat and galoshes which to me was the height of boyhood freedom They had a grandfather or great-grandfather, a very old man we called "Creampuff" who was supposed to have served in the Civil War. Possible, when you think about it.

For all the outward comradeship, I think I was always kind of an outsider. Sports were big in the neighborhood consciousness, and

the Coast Baseball League was pre-eminent prior to the arrival of
the major leagues and the ascendance of other professional sports.
All the kids talked about it and had the batting averages of their
heroes on the San Francisco Seals or Oakland Oaks down pat. Not
wanting to be left out, I memorized everyone's batting averages as
an intellectual enterprise, only to find that they changed the next day,
and again the day after that. It was then I came to the realization that
I really didn't much care about what their batting averages were, or
anything much about professional sports.

We played basketball every time we got near a schoolyard
court. At the top of the hill, though, there were no playgrounds or
schoolyards so most of the time we had to do with what we had.
Our game was step-baseball played against the front steps of houses
on the 2200 block of 22nd. The pink marbled stairs with the sharp
corners were the best.

There wasn't much reading material in the house on 22nd Street
as I remember. There were a few big/little books left over from
the older kids. And later I remember a book of Grimm's Fairytales
and a child's book of illustrated bible stories. But for the most part
I had to satisfy myself with the stories that appeared in the little
weekly Catholic magazine we received in school and the "Treasury
of American Literature," an anthology of short fiction geared to each
grade level. I remember my realization in about the 4th grade that I
had read every story in my reader. I had read a book.

I went on to read the stories in the older kids' readers as well.
But that was about the extent of it. I don't think there was time for
much reading. There was school, then homework, and housework,
after which we were allowed to play outside. In fact, we were
forced to play outside, with orders not to come home until dark,
because Rose Smith didn't want a bunch of kids cluttering up the
house after school.

In 1948, the entire household moved from 3919 22nd Street to
1454 Tenth Avenue where we occupied both of the flats.. I suppose
we moved because the sharp incline from Castro Street up to 3919
was becoming too steep for Rose Smith to climb easily as she got

older. There was another reason, I suspect, as well. The town was changing and it was thought that the Mission District was changing more. It was a time when there was a great deal of concern about postwar juvenile crime. I remember first hearing the term latch-key kid, and learning what the term meant, at 3919. My sense is that Rose wanted to get the younger boys away from the bad influences we would be more likely to encounter there than in the Sunset. Perhaps her concerns were well placed. Most of the kids from around there turned out OK as far as I know with a couple of notable exceptions. A guy we called "Rabbit" who lived up the street on 22nd was one of the five shot (two died) by Robert Ransom at the Butchers' Ball in Civic Center in 1952. That was the last Butchers' Ball, I think, another sign of the changing times. It was customary for all kinds of organizations to host annual balls in large auditoriums, but by the 1950s the fights which tended to break out there put an end to them. It was the same thing with the regular benefit dances held in Larkspur by the Volunteer Fire Department since before the War and which attracted large numbers of young people from the city. By the 1950s they had to be discontinued because of all the fighting. For some reason, our immediate predecessors got along without a lot of public fist-fighting. And Bobby Halligan, from over on Alvarado Street, who we used to hang out with, was arrested and convicted of a robbery/murder at Siri's Market in 1957. (I sold him his first gun, a bb pistol for fifty cents. I spent it all on candy—that was a lot of candy in that economy—and was soon informed by my stomach that more isn't necessarily better when it comes to good things.) Bobby had always been a bit wilder than the rest of us and even earlier we knew he was given to fits of ungovernable rage. Though we lived in the Sunset, I continued at St. Phillips until such time as I could be accepted into St. Anne's. When I think about today's parents who won't let their children out of their sight, I think of the lengthy bus and streetcar trip I took alone back and forth across the city to school daily, sometimes in the dark of early night. Finally I was admitted to St. Anne's where I met friends, some of whom I remain in regular contact with to this day.

St. Anne's was OK., although about this time, based on my experiences I began to doubt the basic Christianity of some of the nuns. I remember being warned of several occasions of sin. One was Rudy's, a little notions store and circulating library on Judah between 9th and 10th.. It was the ideal place for kids to hang out In addition to what could be called adult magazines, the store had comic books and candy as well as other gimcracks which would appeal to kids.

Rudy was a little balding man who always wore a smock and lived in the back of the store. Intimations that there was more to his life than appeared on the surface became apparent when a Jane Russell-type brunette showed up one day to share his backroom and help out at the store. (Many years later, in the 1980s, I ran into Rudy, who then had to have been 90, on the 5th floor of the Hall of Justice. He appeared lost so I introduced myself to him as one of his customers from the 1940s, and offered to direct him to where he wanted to go. He blushingly told me that he was looking for the 6th floor, the city prison floor, because he knew some "young women" up there. It seems that Rudy was still hobnobbing with the girls, even at that advanced age.)

Less defensible was the nuns' caution to stay away from Herman Theriault and Charlie Strom. The only reason we could figure out was that their mothers were divorced single-parents, trying to raise their children alone. I'm sure that the nuns had our best interests at heart, but that can't have been easy on Herman and Charlie. (As a matter of fact, I later got to know Herman's mother, Mrs. T., very well when she provided a sanctuary for the "lost boys" of the neighborhood.)

I always did OK in school if I gave it any effort at all. The problem was that much of time I didn't. In the 8th grade I was relegated to the rows at the left rear of the room which the discipline problems shared with the slow learners. I suppose I was there for some kind of disciplinary problem. One day I was throwing pencils at Bobby Allen whose desk was in the window row. He was throwing them back at me. One pencil bypassed him and went out the window, almost hitting a priest who was walking by. He came to the classroom and, after somehow identifying the culprits, took us to the priest house where he heard our confession. I imagine I had some sense of proportionality even then because I remember thinking that throwing pencils was hardly a confession-level offense.

One day, Sister Cyril McDonald—a good woman and one of the nuns who I remember fondly—kept me after school. (I didn't know it at the time but her police officer father had been murdered in the line of duty at the Crystal Palace Market on 8th Street in the 1930s.) In an effort to influence my behavior for the good, Sister Cyril asked me whether I didn't want to grow up and have a decent family. To accomplish that, she told me I would have to succeed in school. A comic-strip light bulb went off above my head. The nuns were always trolling in those days for likely candidates—those with the academic chops—to steer them to the seminary. I guess I had been listening to the sales pitches because in answer to the good nun's question I said "No." "Then what do you want?" she said. "I want to be a priest," I replied.

Big mistake. Sister hooked right into it and when my father heard about it I was stuck. Having a priest in an Irish family at the time was a feather in the familial cap. There was no going back. I moved, at first willingly, into a new realm, both with teachers and my fellow students. I started attending mass daily. My religious observance, as I look back on it, was obsessive at that period. I was moved over to the "good row" by the window, just behind John Ring and Ron Lambers, both of whom went on to be ordained priests. My grades soared into the mid-90s when I began to apply myself—but not quite as high as those of John and Ron who doubtless had a better foundation, having paid attention to the teachers in earlier years. I changed in the eyes of my fellow students as well. I remember once they picked me to umpire a softball game, about which I probably knew less than most, on the grounds that as a prospective seminarian I would be fair to a fault.

I have sometimes felt bad about tricking Sister Cyril that way because she was a genuinely good woman. I could excuse myself by claiming that I was encouraged down that false path by the vocational suggestions I and my classmates had received from the nuns. On long reflection, however, I thank Sister Cyril for encouraging my "vocation" and have concluded that my stay at the seminary, though I went there flying under false colors, was a positive experience, and one whose memories I treasure to this day. In September 1949, I entered St. Joseph's Minor Seminary at Mountain View. At the entry physical exam I learned that I was 5'1" tall and weighed 100lbs.

Kevin J. Mullen text and photo from THE EGG MAN'S SON, A SAN FRANCISCO IRISH LIFE by Kevin J. Mullen. Reprinted by permission of the author. College Station TX, Virtualbookworm.com Publishing, 2009

❦ *Maya Angelou*

*Escaping racism of one kind, encountering another,
more subtle.*

     In the early months of World War II, San Francisco's Fillmore
district, or the Western Addition, experienced a visible revolution.
On the surface it appeared to be totally peaceful and almost a
refutation of the term "revolution." The Yakamoto Sea Food Market
quietly became Sammy's Shoe Shine Parlor and Smoke Shop.
Yashigara's Hardware metamorphosed into La Salon de Beaute
owned by Miss Clorinda Jackson. The Japanese shops which sold
products to Nisei customers were taken over by enterprising Negro
businessmen, and in less than a year became permanent homes away
from home for the newly arrived Southern Blacks. Where the odors
of tempura, raw fish and cha had dominated, the aroma of chitlings,
greens and ham hocks now prevailed.

The Asian population dwindled before my eyes. I was unable to tell the Japanese from the Chinese and as yet found no real difference in the national origin of such sounds as Ching and Chan or Moto and Kano.

As the Japanese disappeared, soundlessly and without protest, the Negroes entered with their loud jukeboxes, their just-released animosities and the relief of escape from Southern bonds. The Japanese area became San Francisco's Harlem in a matter of months.

A person unaware of all the factors that make up oppression might have expected sympathy or even support from the Negro newcomers for the dislodged Japanese. Especially in views of the fact that they (the Blacks) had themselves undergone concentration-camp living for centuries in slavery's plantations and later in sharecroppers' cabins. But the sensations of common relationship were missing.

The Black newcomer had been recruited on the desiccated farm lands of Georgia and Mississippi by war-plant labor scouts. The chance to live in two-or-three-story apartment buildings (which became instant slums), and to earn two-and even three-figured weekly checks, was blinding. For the first time he could think of himself as a Boss, a Spender. He was able to pay other people to work for him, i.e. the dry cleaners, taxi drivers, waitresses, etc. The shipyards and ammunition plants brought to booming life by the war let him know that he was needed and even appreciated. A completely alien yet very pleasant position for him to experience. Who could expect this man to share his new and dizzying importance with concern for a race that he had never known to exist?

Another reason for his indifference to the Japanese removal was more subtle but was more profoundly felt. The Japanese were not whitefolks. Their eyes, language and customs belied the white skin and proved to their dark successors that since they didn't have to be feared, neither did they have to be considered. All this was decided unconsciously.

No member of my family and none of the family friends ever mentioned the absent Japanese. It was as if they had never owned or lived in the houses we inhabited. On Post Street, where our house

was, the hill skidded slowly down to Fillmore, the market heart of
our district. In the two short blocks before it reached its destination,
the street housed two day-and-night restaurants, two pool halls, four
Chinese restaurants, two gambling houses, plus diners, shoeshine
shops, beauty salons, barber shops and at least four churches. To
fully grasp the never-ending activity in San Francisco's Negro
neighborhood during the war, one need only know that the two
blocks described were side streets that were duplicated many times
over in the eight-to-ten-square-block area.

The air of collective displacement, the impermanence of
life in wartime and the gauche personalities of the more recent
arrivals tended to dissipate my own sense of not belonging. In San
Francisco, for the first time, I perceived myself as part of something.
Not that I identified with the newcomers, nor with the rare Black
descendants of native San Franciscans, nor with the whites or even
the Asians, but rather with the times and the city. I understood the
arrogance of the young sailors who marched the streets in marauding
gangs, approaching every girl as if she were at best a prostitute and
at worst an Axis agent bent on making the U.S..A. lose the war. The
undertone of fear that San Francisco would be bombed which was
abetted by weekly air raid warnings and civil defense drills in school,
heightened my sense of belonging. Hadn't I, always, but ever and
ever, thought that life was just one great risk for the living?

Then the city acted in wartime like an intelligent woman
under siege. She gave what she couldn't with safety withhold, and
secured those things which lay in her reach. The city became for
me the ideal of what I wanted to be as a grownup. Friendly but
never gushing, cool but not frigid or distant, distinguished without
the awful stiffness.

To San Franciscans "The City That Knows How" was the
Bay, the fog, Sir Francis Drake Hotel, Top o'the Mark, Chinatown,
the Sunset District and so on and so forth and so white. To me,
a thirteen-year-old Black girl, stalled by the South and Southern
Black life style, the city was a state of beauty and a state of freedom.
The fog wasn't simply the steamy vapors off the bay caught and
penned in by the hills, but a soft breath of anonymity that shrouded

and cushioned the bashful traveler. I became dauntless and free
of fears, intoxicated by the physical fact of San Francisco. Safe
in my protecting arrogance, I was certain that no one loved her as
impartially as I. I walked around the Mark Hopkins and gazed at
the Top o' the Mark, but (maybe sour grapes) was more impressed
by the view of Oakland from the hill than by the tiered building or
its fur-draped visitors. For weeks, after the city and I came to terms
about my belonging, I haunted the points of interest and found them
empty and un–San Francisco. The naval officers with their well-
dressed wives and clean white babies inhabited another time-space
dimension than I. The well-kept old women in chauffeured cars and
blond girls in buckskin shoes and cashmere sweaters might have
been San Franciscans but they were at most gilt on the frame of my
portrait of the city.

Pride and Prejudice stalked in tandem the beautiful hills.
Native San Franciscans, possessive of the city, had to cope with an
influx, not of awed respectful tourists but of raucous unsophisticated
provincials. They were also forced to live with skin-deep guilt
brought on by the treatment of their former Nisei schoolmates.

Southern white illiterates brought their biases intact to the West
from the hills of Arkansas and the swamps of Georgia. The Black
ex-farmers had not left their distrust and fear of whites which history
had taught them in distressful lessons. These two groups were
obliged to work side by side in the war plants, and their animosities
festered and opened like boils on the face of the city.

San Franciscans would have sworn on the Golden Gate Bridge
that racism was missing from the heart of their air-conditioned city.
But they would have been sadly mistaken.

A story went the rounds about a San Franciscan, a white matron
who refused to sit beside a Negro civilian on the streetcar, even after
he made room for her on the seat. Her explanation was that she
would not sit beside a draft dodger who was a Negro as well.

She added that the least he cold do was fight for his country the
way her son was fighting on Iwo Jima. The story said that the man
pulled his body away from the window to show an armless sleeve.

He said quietly and with great dignity, "Then ask your son to look around for my arm, which I left over there."

Although my grades were very good (I had been put up two semesters on my arrival from Stamps [Georgia]), I found myself unable to settle down in the high school. It was an institution for girls near my house, and the young ladies were faster, brasher, meaner and more prejudiced than any I had met at Lafayette County Training School. Many of the Negro girls were, like me, straight from the South, but they had known or claimed to have known the bright lights of Big D (Dallas) or T Town (Tulsa, Oklahoma), and their language bore up their claims. They strutted with an aura of invincibility, and along with some of the Mexican students who put knives in their tall pompadours they absolutely intimidated the white girls and those Black and Mexican students who had no shield of fearlessness. Fortunately I was transferred to George Washington High School.

The beautiful buildings sat on a moderate hill in the white residential district, some sixty blocks from the Negro neighborhood. For the first semester, I was one of three Black students in the school, and in that rarefied atmosphere I came to love my people more. Mornings as the streetcar traversed my ghetto I experienced a mixture of dread and trauma. I knew that all too soon we would be out of my familiar setting and Blacks who were on the streetcar when I got on would all be gone and I alone would face the forty blocks of neat streets, smooth lawns, white houses and rich children.

In the evenings on the way home the sensations were joy, anticipation and relief at the first sign which said BARBECUE or DO DROP INN or HOME COOKING or at the first brown faces on the street. I recognized that I was again in my country.

In the school itself I was disappointed to find that I was not the most brilliant or even nearly the most brilliant student. The white kids had better vocabularies than I and, what was more appalling, less fear in the classrooms. They never hesitated to hold up their hands in response to a teacher's question; even when they were wrong they were wrong aggressively, while I had to be certain about all my facts before I dared to call attention to myself.

George Washington High School was the first real school I attended. My entire stay there might have been time lost if it hadn't been for the unique personality of a brilliant teacher. Miss Kirwin was that rare educator who was in love with information. I will always believe that her love of teaching came not so much from her liking for students but from her desire to make sure that some of the things she knew would find repositories so that they could be shared again.

She and her maiden sister worked in the San Francisco city school system for over twenty years. My Miss Kirwin, who was a tall, florid buxom lady with battleship-gray hair, taught civics and current events. At the end of a term in her class our books were as clean and the pages as stiff as they had been when they were issued to us. Miss Kirwin's students were never or vary rarely called upon to open textbooks.

She greeted each class with "Good day, ladies and gentlemen." I had never heard an adult speak with such respect to teenagers. (Adults usually believe that a show of honor diminishes their authority.). "In today's *Chronicle* there was an article on the mining industry in the Carolinas (or some such distant subject). I am certain that all of you have read the article. I would like someone to elaborate on the subject for me."

After the first two weeks in her class, I, along with all the other excited students, read the San Francisco papers, *Time* magazine, *Life* and everything else available to me, Miss Kirwin proved Bailey [her stepfather] right. He had told me once that "all knowledge is spendable currency depending on the market."

There were no favorite students. No teacher's pets. If a student pleased her during a particular period, he could not count on special treatment in the next day's class, and that was as true the other way around. Each day she faced us with a clean slate and acted as if ours were clean as well. Reserved and firm in her opinions, she spent no time in indulging the frivolous.

She was stimulating instead of intimidating. Where some of the other teachers went out of their way to be nice to me—to be a "liberal" with me—and others ignored me completely, Miss Kirwin never seemed to notice that I was Black and therefore different. I was Miss Johnson and if I had the answer to a question she posed I was never given any more than the word "Correct," which was what she said to every other student with the correct answer.

Years later when I returned to San Francisco I made visits to her classroom. She always remembered that I was Miss Johnson, who had a good mind and should be doing something with it. I was never encouraged on those visits to loiter or linger about her desk. She acted as if I must have had other visits to make. I often wondered if she knew she was the only teacher I remembered.

I never knew why I was given a scholarship to the California Labor School. It was a college for adults, and many years later I found that it was on the House Un-American Activities list of subversive organizations. At fourteen I accepted a scholarship and got one for the next year as well. In the evening class I took drama and dance, along with white and Black grownups. I had chosen drama simply because I liked Hamlet's soliloquy beginning "To be, or not to be." I had never seen a play and did not connect movies with the theater. In fact, the only times I had heard the soliloquy had been when I had melodramatically recited it to myself in front of a mirror.

It was hard to curb my love for the exaggerated gesture and the emotive voice. When Bailey and I read poems together, he sounded like a fierce Basil Rathbone and I like a maddened Bette Davis. At the California Labor School a forceful and perceptive teacher quickly and unceremoniously separated me from melodrama.

She made me do six months of pantomime.

Bailey and Mother encouraged me to take dance, and he privately told me that the exercise would make my legs big and widen my hips. I needed no greater inducement.

My shyness at moving clad in black tights around a large empty room did not last long. Of course, at first, I thought everyone would be staring at my cucumber-shaped body with its knobs for knees, knobs for elbows and, alas, knobs for breasts. But they really did not notice me, and when the teacher floated across the floor and finished an arabesque, my fancy was taken. I would learn to move like that. I would learn to, in her words, "occupy space." My days angled off Miss Kirwin's class, dinner with Bailey and Mother, and drama and dance.

The allegiances I owed at this time in my life would have made very strange bedfellows. Momma with her solemn determination, Mrs. Flowers and her books, Bailey with his love, my mother and her gaiety, Miss Kirwin and her information, my evening classes of drama and dance.

Our house was a fourteen-room typical San Franciscan post-Earthquake affair. We had a succession of roomers, bringing and taking their different accents, and personalities and foods. Shipyard workers clanked up the stairs (we all slept on the second floor except Mother and Daddy Clidell) in their steel-tipped boots and metal hats, and gave way to much-powdered prostitutes, who giggled through their make-up and hung their wigs on the doorknobs. One couple (they were college graduates) held long adult conversations with me in the big kitchen downstairs, until the husband went off to war. Then the wife who had been so charming and ready to smile changed into a silent shadow that played infrequently along the walls. An older couple lived with us for a year or so. They owned a restaurant and had no personality to enchant or interest a teenager, except that the husband was called Uncle Jim, and the wife Aunt Boy. I never figured that out.

The quality of strength lined with tenderness is an unbeatable combination, as are intelligence and necessity when unblunted by formal education. I was prepared to accept Daddy Clidell as one more faceless name added to Mother's roster of conquests. I had trained myself so successfully through the years to display interest, or at least attention, while my mind skipped free on other subjects that I could have lived in his house without ever seeing him and without his becoming the wiser. But his character beckoned and elicited admiration. He was a simple man who had no inferiority complex about his lack of education and even more amazing, no superiority complex because he had succeeded despite that lack. He would say often, "I been to school three years in my life. In Slaten, Texas, times was hard and I had to help my daddy on the farm."

No recriminations lay hidden under the plain statement, nor was there boasting when he said, "If I'm living a little better now, it's because I treats everybody right."

He owned apartment buildings and later, pool halls, and was famous for being that rarity "a man of honor." He didn't suffer, as many "honest men" do, from the detestable righteousness that diminishes their virtue. He knew cards and men's hearts. So during the age when Mother was exposing us to certain facts of life like personal hygiene, proper posture, table manners, good restaurants and tipping practices, Daddy Clidell taught me to play poker, blackjack, tonk and high, low, Jick, Jack and the Game. He wore expensively tailored suits and a large yellow diamond stickpin. Except for the jewelry he was a conservative dresser and carried himself with the unconscious pomp of a man of secure means. Unexpectedly, I resembled him, and when he, Mother and I walked down the street his friends often said, "Clidell, that's sure your daughter. Ain't no way you can deny her."

Proud laughter followed those declarations, for he had never had children. Because of his late-arriving but intense paternal sense, I was introduced to the most colorful characters in the Black underground. One afternoon, I was invited into our smoke-filled dining room to make the acquaintance of Stonewall Jimmy, Just Black, Cool Clyde, Tight Coat and Red Leg. Daddy Clidell explained to me that they were the most successful con-men in the world, and they were going to tell me about some games so that I would never be "anybody's mark."

To begin, one man warned me, "There ain't never been a mark yet that didn't want something for nothing." Then they took turns showing me their tricks, how they chose their victims (marks) from the wealthy bigoted whites and in every case how they used the victims' prejudice against them.

Some of the tales were funny, a few were pathetic but all were amusing or gratifying to me, for the Black man, the con man who could act the most stupid, won out every time over the powerful, arrogant white. By all accounts those storytellers, born Black and male before the turn of the twentieth century, should have been ground into useless dust. Instead they used their intelligence to pry open the door of rejection and not only became wealthy but got some revenge in the bargain.

It wasn't possible for me to regard them as criminals or be anything but proud of their achievements.

The needs of a society determine its ethics, and in the Black American ghettos the hero is that man who is offered only the crumbs from his country's table but by ingenuity and courage is able to take for himself a Lucullan feast. Hence the janitor who lives in one room but sports a robins-egg-blue Cadillac is not laughed at but admired, and the domestic who buys forty-dollar shoes is not criticized but is appreciated. We know that they have put to use their full mental and physical powers. Each single gain feeds into the gains of the body collective .

Stories of law violations are weighed on a different set of scales in the Black mind than in the white. Petty crimes embarrass the community and many people wistfully wonder why Negroes don't rob more banks, embezzle more funds and employ graft in the unions. "We are the victims of the world's most comprehensive robbery. Life demands a balance. It's all right if we do a little robbing now." This belief appeals particularly to one who is unable to compete legally with his fellow citizens.

My education and that of my Black associates were quite different from the education of our white schoolmates. In the classroom we all learned past participles, but in the streets and in our homes the Blacks learned to drop s's from plurals and suffixes from past-tense verbs. We were alert to the gap separating the written word from the colloquial. We learned to slide out of one language and into another without being conscious of the effort. At school, in a given situation, we might respond with "That's not unusual."

But in the street, meeting the same situation, we easily said, "It be's like that sometimes."

WHY STAY BALD WHEN GROWING HAIR IS SO SIMPLE—By Goldberg

PULL STRING (A) WHICH CAUSES SECONDARY STRING (B) TO MOVE SCISSORS AND CUT ONE HAIR FROM WOODEN HORSE'S TAIL - CLUTCH (E) GRABS HAIR, LIFTS IT AT PULL OF STRING (D) AND DROPS IT IN TUBE (F) - TINCTURE OF IRON DROPS ON HAIR FROM BEAKER (G) - HAIR FALLS INTO HANDS OF TOY-SAILOR (H) WHO TIES A SAILOR'S KNOT ON THE END OF IT - WHEN IT LEAVES SAILOR'S HANDS, FAN (I) BLOWS IT INTO MOUTH OF BALD- HEADED MAN - STRONG ELECTRIC MAGNET (J) PULLS IRON-SOAKED HAIR THROUGH THE TOP OF HIS HEAD - SAILOR'S KNOT PREVENTS IT FROM LEAVING HEAD. OPERATION IS REPEATED UNTIL THERE IS ENOUGH HAIR ON TOP OF HEAD TO COMB.

✎ *Rube Goldberg*

From: Oral History interview with Rube Goldberg, 1970, New York City. Interviewer: Emily Nathan

EN: Mr. Goldberg, I understand the exhibition of your work in Washington is going to go way back into your past. It'll really be an enormous retrospective.

RG: Yes, I'm very pleased. I think it's going to be one of the best things that's…gonna …to be sort of the climax of my career. I don't want to say that it's like looking at your own obituary (laughs) you know, when they glorify somebody…

EN: How did they find the ones you had forgotten?

RG: Well, I don't know. They dug them up , they just uh…Most of my work is at the University of California, in the Bancroft library, which is my alma mater, at Berkeley…
And they have a drawing there that I made when I was twelve years old. I used to go to the…I didn't have any real art training, but when I was about twelve or thirteen, another boy and I went to a sign painter's house every Friday night and took lessons. He was a good painter; he was a sign painter because he had to make a living and we used to go there and, oh, I enjoyed that tremendously and I…

EN: That's wonderful. And it will go into your cartoons and newspaper cartoons.

RG: Oh yes.…I've forgotten so many things. I started doing sports cartoons in 1905, before you were born. And that's the only opening there was for a young cartoonist to get, the sports cartoons or editorial cartoons…so I did sports cartoons.…

RG: I studied engineering because my father thought that all cartoonists were, you know, good-for-nothing, Bohemians, who couldn't make a living drawing pictures…So he was paying for it and he and I got along very well and so, I got a diploma in 1904. And I worked at it six months…when I was…

EN: You knew it was not for you.

RG: Naw. And during my college, at the end of the junior year I worked in a mine, then I knew I was..

EN: As a miner?

RG: Yeah, well , for six weeks I went down two thousand feet, in a gold mine, shoveling, my hands were like ribbons and I said this is not for me. But that was part of the course. I didn't want to say I was afraid, which I was; I was scared to death.

So I did sports cartoons. And my brother sent me a book of clippings of sports cartoons that I made in 1908 and 1909, and they were very interesting. I looked at 'em and I couldn't believe that I did 'em, because I did one every day. It was a half page in the paper.

EN: Ooph, three hundred and sixty-five, well, not quite three hundred and sixty a year, about.

RG: Yeah. I didn't write because in the course I took, mining engineering of all things, you know they graduate a mining engineer as a sort of illiterate. They didn't have any cultural courses at all at that time; they do now. And, when I went to a fight up in Reno, I was working on the San Francisco *Bulletin,* and I went up to a fight in Reno where Jeffries gave away his title in 1905. And I was making cartoons and the fella who was doing the writing, a sports writer, got drunk.

EN: Hmm, that was your good fortune.

RG: See, the editor wired me. He says, "Send in stories." Well, I says, "I don't write, I…" He says, "Send 'em in, right away; anybody can write." So I've been writing off and on ever since.

EN: And when did you start making those wonderful, great contraptions, those machinations?

RG: When I was taking a course in analytic mechanics, the professor had a big machine that each student had to experiment with and get an answer. And you had to find the weight of the earth with this contraption. There was a whole room full of retorts and Bunsen burners and beakers and motors. And, I did that, and there was nothing more ridiculous to me than finding the weight of the earth because I didn't care how much the earth weighed.

EN: [Laughs]

RG: And later on, Uh, I didn't have any idea that this would be…I thought this was very useless, you know. I had no idea that this was going to come in handy in my cartoon work later on. And I didn't know, I just hark back to this thing and say, this is funny, and that's the way people go to a great extreme to accomplish very little.

EN: [Laughs]

RG: So I added midgets and I added stale bullets. I added monkeys; I added incongruous elements. And this was all sort of a kind of a progressive thing you know, like a chain reaction…One thing led to another and then you started with something and you finished with another and, uh, these inventions I incorporated those into my regular cartoons and, for some reason or other they were taken up.. They stood out and I'm typed as an inventor; I'm a crazy inventor

I didn't say this is going to make me famous or this is going to come out the way it did. It just happened that the public happened to appreciate the satirical quality of these crazy things

I knew what I wanted to do, and I knew that I had to make good and I, because I had great doubts about whether I would get to where I wanted to. But I was full of ambition; I did all this work and I was very lucky it came out. I think you have to be very lucky. I'm a great believer..

EN: Yes?

RG: …in luck, not a roulette wheel luck…

EN: Yes…

RG:…but luck in, in connection with your effort

EN: Mmhmm.

RG: I'm still ambitious which sounds kind of silly for a guy eighty-seven years old.

EN: I don't think it sounds silly at all.

RG: And my name is in the dictionary and I'm very pleased.

Rube Goldberg Interview, 1970 by Emily Nathan and cartoon from Archives of American Art, Smithsonian Institution.

❧ *Ernest Lageson*

Making oneself at home. On Alcatraz.

It was a beautiful day in June of 1942 when the letter that changed all of our lives arrived. Dad had accompanied a friend to a farm sale in Egeland, North Dakota, and Mom and I were home alone. In the mail that day there was a letter from the Bureau of Prisons advising of Dad's assignment as a Junior Custodial Officer to Alcatraz Island Prison.

Later that summer we moved into a spacious apartment in Building 64 on Alcatraz. The large stone structure had been used as a barracks during the Army occupation of the island and was remodeled into a 30-40-unit apartment house by the Bureau of Prisons. Our new home consisted of two bedrooms, a living room, bathroom and a kitchen large enough for an eating area in one corner. The apartment was completely furnished except for linen and kitchen utensils. On Dad's new annual salary of $1,860, the $25 per month rent he paid was no financial burden. Soon after moving to Alcatraz, Mom went to work for the Treasury Department in the Alcohol Tax Unit. Her job dealt primarily with federal taxation of California wineries which were then small and principally family-owned. With both of them working, the folks enjoyed the strongest financial position of their lives.

Compared to the prairie, living on an island in the middle of San Francisco Bay was about as extreme a change as one could imagine. After the summer heat and humidity of the Midwest, we were amazed at the cold wind and fog that swirled about our island home. It was customary during heavy fog to keep the inmates in their cells until there was some clearing before sending them down to the work area. Some days there was no clearing and the prisoners left their cells only for meals. While foggy weather prompted fear within the administration of escape attempts, and some did occur, trying to escape in the fog was virtually suicidal. Once away from the island in the fog, an inmate would be totally disoriented, and unable to see landmarks to assist him in reaching the mainland. Every escape attempt in the fog was doomed from the start, and they all failed.

On foggy days, one was keenly aware of the monotonous, booming sound of the foghorns but soon learned to ignore it. The foghorns affected sleep in various ways. If you went to sleep during clear weather, you would probably be awakened if they began to sound in the middle of the night. If you went to sleep listening to them, you would probably be awakened in the middle of the night if the foghorns stopped. And then there were those poor souls who had trouble sleeping at all if the horns were sounding.

Additionally, our lives were controlled by the boat schedule and public transportation since we didn't have a car. Mom and Dad also dealt with the ever-present fear of missing the 12:30 AM boat and being marooned on the San Francisco dock until 6:30 the next morning. In later years the folks laughed about the many movies they did not get to see to conclusion to insure catching that last boat of the night.

Life in the Bay Area was dominated by the war. The City lived under a partial blackout to protect against air or naval attack by the Japanese. All of the street lights in San Francisco were equipped with little caps to direct the light downward to reduce the visibility from aircraft overhead. An anti-submarine net stretched across the Golden Gate to guard the bay from enemy submarines. The net was held in place by large buoys, which from time to time would be brought to Alcatraz by the Coast Guard for maintenance and repair. The work of sandblasting, repairing and repainting the buoys was carried out on the dock and performed by inmate labor. An artillery detachment was stationed on Alcatraz to main the two anti-aircraft batteries mounted on the roof of the cell house and one of the apartment buildings. Military bases were scattered all around the bay, and military personnel were everywhere. As a youngster living on Alcatraz, I had no fear of the prisoners, but lived in constant fear that we would be the victims of hostile military activity. It was a time of ultra-patriotism, when everyone was totally dedicated to winning the war. Military personnel were appreciated and respected and the entire nation was united in our defense against the Axis powers.

The island operated somewhat as a military society with rank and seniority having its privileges. The day to day grocery needs were met by the canteen, a small grocery store operated by the Officers' Club. The island boat schedule of 12-15 trips per day was augmented by the Army boat from Angel Island, which made travel to and from the City fairly convenient. The island had its own post office which was operated by the wife of one of Dad's closest friends.

Island social activities were held in the social hall. These included potluck dinners, parties during the holidays and various club, Red Cross, and similar meetings throughout the year. Alcoholic beverages were not permitted on the island, however this rule was adhered to more in its violation than its observance. In fact, during the time he lived with us, Grandpa McLean had his own method of evading the law. He would take me with him shopping in the City. In addition to his other purchases, he would buy several bottles of beer and have me carry the beer bag on the boat to avoid observation. Fishing was popular and after the inmates were locked up for the evening, unlimited fishing was permitted from the dock.

Recreation activities for the adults included bowling on the two lanes on the lower floor of the social hall. There were also pool and billiard tables there. The boys on the island worked as pin-setters for the bowling leagues organized by the adults. We worked one to a lane and set the pins by hand. We were paid ten cents a line, which meant that on a good night you could earn two or three dollars. At one point, some of the older boys decided they needed a raise and when their demands were rejected, they called a strike. This was totally ignored by the officers, who set their own pins and saved the dime a line they had been paying us. In short order the younger boys, myself included, realized we had made a mistake and returned to work at the previous rate.

Life as a child on Alcatraz was pleasant and easy. I had many friends and there was always plenty to do. We attended school in San Francisco and I developed another circle of friends there. We were free to have our school friends visit us on the island and this happened frequently. The games we played usually related to the war, with the boys playing the role of combatants and the girls as nurses In addition to our war games in which we always defeated the "Japs" or the Germans, prison was a popular game among the boys. An area under one of the stairways was the prison and of course, the "cons" were always trying to escape. There were also the periodic, beach-combing trips to out-of-the-way sections of the island's rocky coast in search of "neat stuff" that frequently washed ashore. Just sitting on the seawall observing ships entering and leaving the bay was a pleasant experience for the observer of any age. The bay, the ship traffic, and the view was never the same, always interesting and beautiful. The bay was teeming with warships, sleek destroyers, majestic cruisers, daunting aircraft carriers, troop transports en route to the South Pacific, and merchant ships from all over the world.

Not surprisingly, toy weapons were not permitted on the island. Facsimile guns, knives, swords, clubs, even water pistols were strictly forbidden. Since whistle signals were used to control inmate movement in the cell house, toy whistles were also prohibited. Because of space limitations, dogs, cats, and large pets were not permitted. Fish, turtles, hamsters, and anything that lived in a bowl or a cage were acceptable.

Occasionally during winter storms, the bay waters became too rough for small boat traffic and the launch did not run. That meant no school for the children. Once we were isolated on the island for two days during a storm and the launch was moored to a pier in San Francisco to protect it from the turbulent waters around the island

On weekends my friends and I would go to town for a movie or just to hang out. My best friend and I belonged to a cub scout pack which met at my grammar school, Sherman. The meetings were in the evening and we would walk from the dock to and from the school at Franklin and Union Streets.

For much of the time that I lived on the island, I was the Alcatraz paperboy. In those days San Francisco had four major newspapers, and I would deliver the morning papers before leaving for school and the afternoon papers as soon as I got home. Twice daily, as part of my route, I would visit the soldiers' living quarters atop the new apartment house. In the morning, there was always something interesting going on, and they would share their breakfast with me. Their meals were prepared on the mainland and delivered three times a day in large thermos boxes. I thought their food, actually very basic, was wonderful.

I was also the warden's errand boy, and made trips to the city to pick up grocery items for him not sold in the canteen. This would involve a trip to the North Point Market in North Beach. For this I was paid a dollar, generous pay for the time.

During the very infrequent prison break attempts, there was understandable concern among the women and children of the island, since they all had husbands and fathers who would be involved should serious difficulties arise. The standing order on the island was that in the event of an escape attempt, those of the civilian population were to return to their apartments, and lock their doors. When the escape siren sounded, that is exactly what happened.

Inmate transfers always arrived on a special boat run. Prisoners and island residents never shared the same boat, so whenever the boat left the island at other than a regularly scheduled time, it meant something special, usually a prisoner shipment. When the boat returned from a special run, the balconies of Building 64 were lined with curious observers. The officers were interested to see how many new inmates were arriving, and if any returnees were among them. The rest of the residents were merely curious. Such shipments were known as "chains" since the inmates arrived in handcuffs and leg irons chained together in a single line. Upon arrival they were loaded on a truck for the trip "up top" to be "dressed in" as official Alcatraz prisoners.

The "new fish" (first time Alcatraz inmates), were always quiet and apprehensive. At the north entrance to the cell house, the new prisoners stepped down from the truck and stood silently in single files. One by one they were taken into the cell house where their shackles and civilian clothes were removed, and they began the indoctrination process. Whoever they were, or thought they were, in their prior institution, at Alcatraz, each was just another number. His prison career was starting all over, and he was on the bottom rung of a very austere social ladder.

In North Dakota, I had attended a small school containing grades one through twelve, where everyone knew everyone; but in San Francisco things were entirely different. Sherman had a student body of 250-300 and was kindergarten through sixth grade. On the first day of school as a fifth-grader, I went to school without any parental help, accompanied by other Alcatraz kids. Once we arrived, they all disappeared and I was on my own.

Being a student at Sherman brought me quickly into the urban world. I was exposed for the first time to mentally and physically handicapped children who attended special classes, but were with us during part of the school day. There were also a few non-English-speaking students whom we were expected to assist in learning the language. I recall a Spanish-speaking boy to whom I was assigned with the instruction to help him learn English. I became involved in competitive sports for the first time. In general, I was very much on my own in getting to and from school and carrying out my daily activities.

I remember the enormous pride I felt to have my father join the Navy even though Dad's enlistment brought profound change to the lives of all of us. In June of 1944, in anticipation of military service, he gave up the Alcatraz residence and we moved to an apartment on Sacramento Street.

The new living arrangements were definitely a step down for me. Housing was at a premium and we were lucky to find an apartment. 1875 Sacramento Street was a twelve-unit apartment building. Just off the lobby was a tiny room large enough to hold a single bed. This was my sleeping room for about six months.

My transformation from an Alcatraz kid to a City kid was immediate. With my paper route, I was on the street daily, meeting new friends, learning the neighborhood and becoming part of city life.

In April of 1945, representatives of fifty nations met in San Francisco to draft the charter of the United Nations. By that time, it was clear that the Allied forces would prevail and that the end of the war was only a matter of time. My friends and I were among the crowds that lined the streets around the Opera House, where the meetings were being held. Although we were only children, we all knew that something historic was taking place and we wanted to be part of it. At the same time, we were fascinated by the flowing robes of the Arabs, the saris and turbans of the Indians, and the many different uniforms from around the world.

Ernest Lageson, from LAGESON LEGACY, a memory, 2008, and GUARDING THE ROCK, by Ernest Lageson, Sr. and Ernest Lageson, Golden Gate Nation Park Conservancy, 2010. Photgraph courtesy of Ernest Lageson.

❧ *John Patrick Diggins*

From the beer gardens to the groves of academe

Jack Diggins was either the best historian who ever played basketball, or the best basketball player who ever wrote history.

The two disciplines informed each other, and helped produce an extraordinary man.

We both grew up in San Francisco, a great city that is also a small town. A compact place where people know each other and tend to remain in touch even as their lives expand outward and to exist and sometimes excel in more than one discipline. Jack was, and remains, one of us.

He was an outstanding basketball player, who'd developed a great lefthanded jumpshot at Argonne Playground in the Richmond District. In those days, Catholic and public high schools competed in the same league, and Jack, as a shooting guard and great defensive player for Sacred Heart High was one of the league's stars. He was named to the San Francisco All-City team, and also the All Northern California team. At the annual all high school tournament in Gridley, California, Jack was named the most valuable player. Twelve years ago Jack was inducted into the Sacred Heart Sports Hall of Fame, joining some fairly illustrious members: among them Gentleman Jim Corbett, former Heavyweight Champion of the World. At the induction ceremony, no one even bothered to mention Jack's academic career.

His friends knew better. We were part of a group, thirty or forty of us, jocks or wanna-be's, from different schools, who gathered every Friday night at an old-man's card-playing area in Golden Gate Park we re-christened The Beer Gardens. We drank beer, talked and argued: sports, politics, religion, women, books, music and movies. Ideas were prized, and you had to be able to defend yours with wit, acuity, perception and rhetoric.

This was the fifties, a stiflingly conformist time—the cold war at its chilliest, a universal draft, McCarthyism—when to be a young man was to be a cipher. There was no youth culture, so we assembled our own. Everybody read, even the slow kids—Mickey Spillane, *The Amboy Dukes*. For music, we relied on an all-black radio station where they played what was then called rhythm and blues. We were tested, by guys from other schools, other cultures, and in the process became something other than our parents' sons, our coaches' players. It's where, I believe, Jack developed his initial suspicion of authority, his skepticism toward received opinion, and what I would call his intellectual athleticism, a basketball-like compound of agility, quickness and determination. He learned to drive to the hole.

The closest approximation to what we had is probably the movie "Diner". But we were both earlier and more anarchic than that. After a minimal six beers at the Beer Gardens, we would go out into the city looking for parties or dances, to few of which we were invited. The declared goal would be women or adventure, but the real purpose was a story, to be shaped, rounded, and perhaps embellished at the Beer Gardens.

One night when Jack was trying out for Pete Newell's
University of California Golden Bears, we tried to crash a party
and ended up getting crashed instead. I never even got in the door.
Jack was pushed or thrown down a flight of stairs and injured his
leg. We rushed him to Harbor Emergency Hospital.. He had broken
his ankle and a pin had to be inserted in it. His big-time basketball
career was over.

Jack had always been bright, but not especially studious. But
he had always been an introspective basketball player, always
thinking one step ahead of the play. Now, unable to play serious
basketball he transferred his athletic diligence and demanding
performance standards to school. There was a professor at Cal
teaching a new discipline, Intellectual History. Jack enrolled in the
class, and was hooked.

The rest, in more than one sense, is history: sixteen books,
a National Book Award nomination, visiting professorships at
Princeton and the Sorbonne, a distinguished professorship at the
Graduate Center at the City University of New York.

Looking back, I would have to say that many people would
call what we were a gang. But there were no drugs, no weapons,
no innocent people preyed upon. And some unusual and even
useful men emerged from who and what we were, with Jack as the
prime example. Through his work, he continues to speak for the
best in all of us.

Not long ago I went with my daughter and her infant twins
to the site of the Beer Gardens. It's a quiet place now, a secluded
dell with tables marked out for chess. There were no other people
around, so my daughter, who had noticed her kids were hungry,
decided to nurse them. I told her I could absolutely swear on the
heads of my grandchildren that this was the first time such a thing
had happened here.

I return now to our original question:

Was Jack Diggins the best historian who ever played basketball,
or the best basketball player who ever wrote history?

The correct answer, in this appropriately reflective setting is: both of the above.

I will close with two stories. The first is from Roy Steiner, who took Chemistry with Jack at Sacred Heart High. Their teacher was Brother Leopold, a notoriously strict Christian Brother, and a very tough grader. Brother Leopold gave no A's, few B's, mostly C's, and both Roy and Jack got D's. They both went to see Brother Leopold to see if they could somehow make up their grades. "We both want to go to College," they told him. Brother Leopold replied, "You guys shouldn't even think about college."

When last heard of, Brother Leopold was supposedly washing bottles at the Christian Brothers Winery in the Napa Valley.

The other story is from Jim Stephens, who played basketball with Jack at City College of San Francisco. Jack was the starter, a guy named Al Holder backed him up, and Jim was third-string. One day, just before a game, the coach came to Jim and told him he was starting. Jim said "Thanks. But how come?" The coach told him the other players had requested it. Jim went to Holder and thanked him. "I'd never do that for you," he said. It was Jack, who'd gone to the coach and suggested that another player start in his place. When Jim told me this story, he said, "That was Digs (which was what we called him then)."

Indeed it was. And it still is.

John Patrick Diggins by John van der Zee, memorial service for John Patrick Diggins, The Graduate Center, City Univerity of New York, 2009. Photo courtesy of Elizabeth Harlan.

✎ *Gus Lee*

Fighting and friendship in the Panhandle

The Panhandle and the Haight, our mirror 'hood south of
the park, were standard-issue wartime blue-collar districts where
shipyard workers and longshoremen returned after back-busting,
long-shift days at Hunters Point and Fort Mason. The Handle and
the Haight were in the sunbelt, unique San Francisco districts without
fog, thunderstorms, or people of Chinese or Caucasian descent.

When I arrived squalling—no doubt prescient about my
imminent fate—the streets were half black. By the time I was in
the second grade and in the center of the frying pan, I was the only
Asian, the only nonblack and the only certified no-question-about-it
nonfighter in the district. Black families, tired of being hammered by
the weight of history and pressured by the burden of being members

of the wrongly hued tribe in Georgia and Mississippi, were heading west armed with hope and cheap gas.

That same hope brought my family trekking eastward on a U.S. Navy Liberty ship called the *USS George Randall*, which my sisters, accustomed to great wealth but sobered by war, regarded as the *Queen Elizabeth.* My father's service as infantry liaison to the China-Burma-India Theatre and Army Ground Forces Commander, Joseph "Vinegar Joe" Stilwell, had earned him a place in the general's heart and berths for our family on an American airplane and a naval vessel.

These families from Macon and Kiangsu met in the Panhandle, a new and voguish rendezvous point for those interested in building life from the rubble of sundered cultures.

Our families arrived gasping, recoiling from shock, happy to be alive but unsure about all else. There was a feeling that something was owed them for this outrageous upset, for nothing that had been done during the preceding years could have justified the insult of war, the hidden costs of relocation, the tariffs of change, the loss of life.

Blacks, for more than a hundred years, had been fighting and bleeding under their nation's flag, hoping for a share of the fruits of victory. They had all the optimism of Dickens's Mr. Micawber, with none of his chances.

During that same century, the Chinese were beset by government corruption, foreign invasion, civil, religious and ethnic wars, revolution, famine, drought, flood, and excess population. They had suffered countless blights. The Taiping rebellion, whose fourteen years of steady siege coincided with the American Civil War, had killed 60 million people. Foreign powers ruled China's coast and imported opium to pay for exports. Legalized opium was laying waste the aristocracy, splintering the social fabric, and threatening even those too poor to purchase it.

China, of course, is not what a billion people call their own country It is *Chung Gwo,* the Middle Kingdom, the central state, the center of the universe, the axis of the world, the home of the celestial heaven's chosen people. It is the home of the tamers of dragons, the sailors of the sea, the students of the moon. Until the eighteenth century, its armies and navies did their will, needing only whim to lash out with lance and sword to carve new boundaries and conquer new worlds.

A rail-thin nine-year-old named Toussaint LaRue looked on during my beatings and only hit me once. I therefore assumed that he occupied some lower social niche than mine. Like a snail's.

He took no pleasure in the China Boy rituals. He instead talked to me. I suspected that he had devised a new method of pain infliction.

"Toussaint," he said, offering his hand. "Ya'lls supposed to shake it." Toussaint would become my guide to American boyhood.

My primary bond to him was for the things he did not do. He did not pound or trap me. He never cut me down. Or laughed with knives in his eyes. Then he opened his heart by explaining things to me, giving me his learning, and taking me into his home.

"China. Don be cryin no mo. Don work on dis here block, no sir, Cap'n! Give 'er up. When ya'll cry, hol' it insida yo'self. Shif' you feet an air-out, go park-side. Preten ya'll gone fishin. Don run, now. Ain't cool."

"Fish in park?" I asked

"Cheez! Ya'll don colly nothing! Ferget da fish, China. Dry yo' tears."

He told me about the theory of fights. That kids did it because it was how you became a man later on.

"Momma tole me," he said, "in ole days, no Negro man kin hit or fight. We belongs to da whites, like hosses.

"Man fight 'notha man, he damaging white man goods. So he get whipped. An I mean *whipped.*" He shook his head and rubbed the top of it, easing the pain of the thought.

"Now, ain't no mo' dat." He said, smiling. We kin fights, like men." He was speaking very seriously. Fighting was a measure of citizenship. Of civilization. I didn't think so.

"China, stan up."

"Why?" I whined.

"Putchur fists up. Make a fist! Right. Bof han's
"Dis one---,"he said, holding my left. "It's fo' guardin yo' face.
Dis here one—dat's fo' poundin da fool who call ya out. Here comes
a punch, and ya'll block it. "China—you listenin ta me?"
"No fight, no reason!" I said hotly.
"No reason?" he yelled. "You can fight wif no *reason*? Boy!
What-chu *talkin* about?"
Uh-oh, I thought. Toussaint's hands were on his hips.
"Evera kid on dis here block like to knock you upside da head
and make you *bleed* and ya'll got no *reason*? China. Ain't no dude
in da Handle got mo' cause fo' fightin *evera* day den *you*!"
"Too many boy fight," I said, drawing back from his heat.
"Uh-uh! No sir, Cap'n! big-time nossir! Lissen. Some kids,
dey fight hard. But ain't never gonna be no gangin up on one kid.
Dat ain't cool." He shook his head. "Kid stan on his feet. No one
else feet. Ain't nobody gonna stan inaway a dat. An youse best
colly dat."
" Hittin' long," I tried.
"Say what?" he said.
"Long. Not light!"
"Wrong? Ya'll say fightin's wrong?"
"Light," I said.
"Howzat?"
"Bad yuing chi," I explained.
"Say *what*?'
"Bad, uh, karma! I said, finding the East Indian word often used
by my sisters.
"Well China, ya'll thinks awful funny. Don have nothing ta
do wif no *caramels*. No matta Big Willie take yo' candies. Ain't
candies. It not bein *chicken*. Not bein yella. Ya'll don havta like it.
Sakes, China, no one like ta Fist City. Well, maybe Big Willie, he
like it. But like it or don like it, no matter none. Ya'll jus *do* it."
He invited me to play in his house. Many of the games
involved capturing cockroaches. "Ya'll ready?" he would ask, and I
would nod, nervously. Toos would kick the wall next to the sink, and
roaches would slither out of the dust and the cracked plaster. Toos

would use his plastic cup, smacking it quickly onto the floor, smiling as he watched the captured roach's antennae struggle to escape, its hard body clicking angrily against the plastic.

He made his closest buddies tolerate me. His mother took me to the church of Reverend Jones on Sundays until my stepmother Edna changed my religion. The simple presence of his company, and that of his pals, saved me from innumerable trashings and gave me time to breathe.

I had never had a friend before, and I cared for him as few lads have for another. My heart fills now when I think of him. That will never change.

Toussaint was, next to me, the skinniest kid on the block. He ran no faster than I since he lacked the sincerity of my efforts, but he was as tough as a slum rat and had the guts of Carmen Basilio. Basilio, the big-headed middleweight who fought while his blood ran down his bruised face like cascading crimson rain in a summer monsoon. Basilio, whose busted face was on the front page of every pinned-up sports section in every barbershop in the city. Kids respected bravery above all else. It was what allowed you to put your pants on in the morning.

My courage was so low that putting on my big-boy underpants was a task. Toussaint was deemed crazy to buddy with me. But he was my friend because I needed one. He got nothing for himself, in the hard world of our peers' respect, for his generosity.

Outside of a table service, we had few possessions, and less cash, but Toos's home made ours look like a gilded palace of Babylon. The La Rue family lived in a windowless converted storage room in a shambling tenement on Masonic, next door to Brook's Mortuary. The stone steps to the main door were chipped, crumbling and dangerous for old people and toddlers. The entryway was a garbage dump for rotted food, and the stairways reeked of old and pungent uric acid.

A sad, small alcoholic named Sippy Suds lived next door to Toussaint. Suds' apartment produced the worst smell in the Panhandle, a rancid sour waft of vomit and urine so strong in the closed space of the hallway that it made you crazy with the badness of it. He used to mess on himself. Suds was one of several people in the 'hood whose speech evaded understanding. I thought it was related to my eyes. Whenever I concentrated and tried to fight through his thick, inebriated Mississippi babble, my eyes watered from the pungent toxins in the air. Suds had everything no one wanted, down to flies that liked his clothes and odors that would cause others to change jobs.

Many of the kids on the block despised Suds, taking his pitiful coins by incessant begging.

"C'mon, Suds, gimme nickel. Yeah! Gimme dollah!"

Toussaint respected him.

"Leave da man be," he said to a whole battalion of yammering kids."Ain't cool, taking poor man's coins. C'mon! Back off!" he shouted, pushing them back. "'Sides. Man yoosta be a fighta," he said.

Heck, I thought. *Everyone* around here is a fighter.

I had seen dead rats before in our house, looking pitiful and scary in the traps, their little feet tucked up in death, thick round tails looking like remnants of ancient lizards. But I had never seen families of them alive. They were on Toussaint's stairs, sluggish, bunched up, and squeaky, and the first time I saw them I stopped and cried. Toussaint looked at me, nodding his head. The rats were pushy and one ran over my foot, small, heavy, sharp-clawed and warm.

"Won hurtcha none," he said, taking my arms as I began to faint.

An elderly and toothless woman lived in a shamble of newspapers and produce cartons on the top of the stairs in the hall. Toussaint called her Missus Hall. She wore old shawls, discarded and unmatched men's shoes, and staggered on broken hips with wriggling loose shoelaces, aided by a short stick wrested from a fruit crate. She would sit on the neighborhood stoops, her crackled fingers pulling splinters from each other, her aged and wrinkled face scrunched with the effort of finding the torment in her hands. During these efforts, her fleshy nose could touch her lips. She was missing clumps of hair, eyelashes, eyebrows. Missus Hall did not look like somenhone who had been very pretty in her youth. But her durability, her will to survive, were attractive, and I liked her very much.

My mother had been beautiful. And she had died.

Missus Hall would relieve herself on old newspapers in the alleyways on Central Avenue. She never spoke to anyone but would nod at Toussaint, who brought her shares of their meager food. The La Rue and the Ting families did not look even a little bit alike, but we had the same caloric intake, while enjoying strong differences on the meaning of Christian charity.

Mrs. LaRue offered to feed me as well, and I was inclined to eat anything that wasn't going to run away from me. This easily included plain, unbuttered grits, which resembled *tze*, rice gruel. But Toussaint's friends never took food from his mother. Her son was too thin.

One Halloween night, after I had been friends with the LaRues for more than five years, Missus Hall smiled at me. I remember that when she showed her teeth I thought she was angry. It took a moment to realize that she was greeting me with a smile, and I beamed back at her, offering her witches' teeth candy, the world full of light.

I asked Mrs. LaRue why Missus Hall never spoke.

"I honestly don't know, Kai," she said. "I figure something almighty drastic happened in her life, and it probly happened twice. Once early, and once late. She's not gonna do nothin fancy with her life. She's jes getting ready for the next blow."

The LaRue home had no furniture, only milk cartons and fruit crates that his momma got from the Reliance Market.

Toussaint had no toys and never asked to play with those belonging to others. He had no father. His mother was wonderful and caring and had convinced Toos that toys and living fathers were not necessary in this mysterious physical world. She carried the whole load, all the way. Toussaint had the gift of love, and they shared everything they had. I was testament to that fact. His smile, shining from a high-cheekboned, high-foreheaded, almost skull-like face, was beatific and had the force of the Prophet. I thought he was the handsomest boy in the world.

As a streetfighter, Toussaint was unusual. He cared nothing for style, which was becoming an extremely big deal to the others.

"Toos," said Jerome Washington. "Y'all fights like a ole' lady. Ya'll fights like Missus Hall." He giggled. "Ain't dat right, Toos?"Jerome was not looking for a fight. He just enjoyed stirring feces with his tongue.

"Dat probly be true, Jerome," said Toussaint, slowly. He was smiling, frustrating Jerome in some mysterious way. Jerome cursed and moved on.

"See, China? Jerome don mess wif me. He wanna hurt mah feelins and I jus talk blahdee-blah trash back at 'em. 'China Bashers.' Dat's a lota crap. Misser Pueblo, in Cutty's Garage. He tole me: fight fo' da fight. Don pay no mind ta no lookers. Style, dat for girls."

"Fists. Be fo' da boy dookin Fist City wif ya."

Toos threw unending series of berserk punches, ignoring incoming rounds as if they were raindrops on a pleasant spring day. He would punch until the fight was over—until Toussaint collapsed or the other kid stopped. I didn't know how he could do that.

When he fought, the smile beat feet, and he became all business. He did not have to do this often. It usually occurred when a Haight kid crossed the border of Fell Street and strutted north up Masonic, looking to break some bones.

Toos's home was on the cross-'hoods thoroughfare. It was Indian Country; trouble came calling with the rising sun.

Toos was skinny and occasionally got picked. He would stand up straight, like an older boy, and roll his shoulders back, like a grown man. He would measure the challenge, giving the Handle crosser a chance to move on. Sometimes his quiet, unfearing gaze was as articulate as my mother's face. When parley failed, he met aggression with his own fury. He was never called out twice by the same youth.

The Haight, six blocks south, was boogeymanland. Boys carried knives, men had zip guns, and women looked more dangerous than twenty San Juan streetfighters with switchblades. Some of the Haight boys wore old –skinned Big Ben coveralls and carried barber shaving razors in the cup of the hand, hiding the flash of steel inside their arm-swaying struts. They could punch a guy and move on. It took a moment to realize that the face had been opened, blood everywhere, the searing pain following long moments after the incision.

"Ya'll stay outa dere," said Toussaint, pointing with a long and skinny thumb at our rival 'hood. "Be boogeymen, big-time."

Until I learned English, I understood it as The Hate.

The Panhandle lay between our 'hoods like no-man's-land, a DMZ that operated without U.N. intervention. Panhandle boys entered the park with great care and only in daylight. It was a jungle of thick eucalyptus, corpses, tangled azalea, and memories of aimless nocturnal screams. Men gathered there at night to smoke and drink and discuss this new land of California. When they disagreed, people died.

The Haight was largely populated by trekkers from Alabama and Louisiana. Mrs. LaRue said their heartaches came from not having a minister. Reverend M. Stamina Jones had followed the LaRues, the Joneses, the Scotts, and the Williamses—the Panhandle families—from Georgia. Others in the neighborhood hailed from Mississippi, Maryland and Tennessee. I thought they were names of streets.

"No ministers in the Haight, just knife fighters," she said. "They'se lost. Toussaint LaRue and Kai Ting, you listen to Momma! Don't be goin into the Haight, no how and no way. Now. *That* be gospel."

Toussaint taught me about music. He tried to translate the world of the chorus in the church of Reverend Jones, but I always suspected that he lacked certainty in his explanations. But he knew that the chorus moved me, and would rub the hair on my head whenever I found myself weeping in time with its singing. I did not have to be an Imperial Scholar to know that crying in this temple house was accepted; the congregation's choral majesty was salted with tears and accented by open weeping. Sobs often served as confirmation of the truth of Reverend Jones's ministry. A dry-eyed assembly meant that his delivery was off the mark.

Toos also introduced me to Mr. Carter, who owned Evil the bulldog. Mr. Carter was a shipyard worker at Hunters Point who lived across the street from us, with the LaRue home around the corner. He had a platoon of ex-wives, no prospects of any more, two radios and a record player, and everyone on the block liked him while hating his dog.

Evil was moody. Somedays he raised his black-and-white head to you on a loose leash, anxious for a pet, his eyes half-closed, his teeth looking sadly overused and brownishly old.

Other days he growled, the fangs angry and huge and brightly wet. He would run around like a broken top with his jaws open, all the kids screaming as they scattered. Evil never caught me; I was the flight expert. He would clamp his maws around a kid's leg and throw his neck back and forth and Mr. Carter would blow that whistle in Evil's ear until he let go. He would then use a fat clothes-hanger dowel to beat the starch out of the dog, and I was the only one who felt sorry for him.

"Oughta jes give dat dog away," said Toos. I shook my head. "Give doggie mo' food," I said. "He too much hungry."

"China, you'se a very funny boy," he said. "Now. Don let no dog smell yo' fear. He smell dat, he get feared hisself and eat yo' pants in a *big* hurry."

The men who had been in the army would sit on the wide stairs of Mr. Carter's place and sing "What the Best-Dressed Man in Harlem Is Wearing Tonight," "The Blues in the Night," and I could close my eyes and sway to their unearthly beautiful voices. They also sang songs they called Jodies. I knew them, my father used to chant them while he chopped vegetables in the kitchen when our mother was still alive.

"Yo'momma was dere when ya lef"
"YO RIGHT!"
"Jody was dere when ya lef"
"YO' RIGHT!"
"Sound off—"

"ONE-TWO!"
"Sound off—"
"THREE-FO!"
"Bring it on down---"
"ONE-TWO-THREE-FO!"
"ONE-TWO-THREE-FO!"

"Jody got somethin dat you ain't got"
"I'S BIN SO LONG AH ALMOS' FO'GOT"
"Yo' baby's as lonely as lonely can be"
"WIF ONLY JODY FO'COM-PANY'"
"Ain't it great to have a pal"
'TA HELP KEEP UP HER MO-RALE'
"Sound off..."
"Yo' not gonna get out till da enda da war"
'IN NINET'IN HUNDRA' AN' SEVENTYFOUR..."

Adults and kids gathered on Mr. Carter's stoop to sing and clap hands, or to gently swing to "Harlem Nocturne" and the high throaty jazz of Billie Holiday's "Strange Fruit," "The Way You Look Tonight," and "God Bless the Child." Toos told me that the words to that song meant that if God did not love you, you were soon dead, because little came to short people without God's grace.

"Good news is, China," said Toos, "dat God love all chilun."

"Me, too?" I asked.

"Dat gotta be true," he said. "God get dibs on all da little chilun he kin find. And," he said, elbowing me, "you're little."

We would keep time and tap with one foot while keeping the other ready to exit stage left if Evil felt the urge. The muse didn't come cheap in the Panhandle.

"Mista Carter," said Toussaint's mom, "that's not right, naming a dog Evil. You can come up with a better name'n that. I know you can. Callin something a name sometime make it so."

"Charlotte, you think it be a big favor to all de chilun on dis block be comin up ta dis here dog and callin 'em *Spot?* Or *Fido?*

See. His firs' name, it was Winston. The name offered no warnin. Folks like ta pet 'em. Den he start to eat kids. He gots too much crust. I call 'em what he is: Evil." He whacked his pants leg with the dowel.

Kids learned to make their own music, without radios. I thought this was because of Evil, since the price of listening to radios could be a pint of dog-drawn blood. But I was wrong. Kids, even poor and unhappy ones, love to sing, warbling the purity of expression, the unsullied and miraculous poetry of a child's honesty. Happy kids sing better. Toos sat on his crumbling steps with Titus McGovern and Alvin Sharpes—boys who had pledged their lives to him—to sing the "Papa Ditty," and other rapadiddle tunes from the not-so-distant South.

"Well, I don know but I been tole,
Papa gonna buy me a pile a coal.
If dat coal don burn fo' me,
Papa gonna take me to da sea.
If dat sea don make me wet,
Papa gonna sink us deeper in debt.
If dat debt don eat our food,
Papa gonna thank da good Saint Jude."

And so on.

Each kid would sing a two-line stanza, making it up as he went. I always shook my head, lowering it as I blushed when it was my turn.

"Dang!" cried Alvin Sharpes. "Lookit China's face. It all red! How you do dat, China?" It was easy. I couldn't rhyme.

"Missa LaRue," I asked, struggling to align the L's and the R's. "Kin rearn me 'Papa Ditty'?"

"The 'Papa Ditty'? I don't think I know that, Kai. Can you sing a little of it for me?"

I tried. She laughed and hugged me.

"Oh, sweetnin, that's "The Mockingbird's Song.' Listen to me," she said, bending over, her smoothly angular and pretty face

bright with life, looking at me with a great smile, singing in a deep
mystic voice that scratched the itches in my heart.
"Well, I'll tell you what I've learned.
Papa's gonna buy me a mockingbird.
If that mockingbird don't sing,
Papa's gonna buy me a diamond ring.
If that diamond ring don't shine,
Papa's gonna buy me a bottle of wine.
If that bottle of wine don't pour,
Papa's gonna take us to the shore..."

"My momma rike shore, rike ocean," I said.
"Well, Kai, that big blue sea, it's somethin, all right."

Toussaint told me that Big Willie Mack, the glandular error
in the guise of a twelve-year-old, had been the first to punch me in
my inaugural day on the street.   Big Willie was the toughest dude
on the block, a bad combination of vicious clothes-taking bully
and mean, gutsy fighter.
Toussaint had hit me on the arm that day with that
second, harmless blow, to make sure that Willie didn't wind up
and do it again.
"China, ya'lls gotta fight. Pretty soon, he be takin yo' clothes."
"No. Crows too small. Him long size." I said.
"China. He don't take 'em ta wear. He take 'em to *take em.*
You'se gotta punch it out wif him, China."
"Ohnry make worse, mo' hit."
"Den you hit back mo'. Dat how it is. It hard be livin, be a
stand-up-boy on dis here block, y'all don fight. Don havta *win*, jes
fight. Make it so's da other boy think fightin you's too much work!
Make it easy of *bof* of us."
"Kin you whip Big Wirry?" I asked.
"Nah, don think so. But he know I fights 'em, won give in. He
wan *my* shoes, he gonna havta give me some *blood.*"

I loved Superman and Mighty Mouse. I began to imagine myself as a fighter. Who did good for others and beat the crap out of bad guys. Good karma. I projected myself into the cartoon sequences. I was unconquerable. Here I come to save the day…It means Mighty Mouse is on his way…

After a pounding on the street, I would take out my comics and pore over them with shaking hands and a teary face, trying desperately to incorporate their messages into my body. But the correspondence-school method of street fighting proved unsuccessful.

Then I tried reason. Be pal? I would offer. Pow! I don wan twubble wit you. Wham! Here, candy? Snatch!

Forget reason. I returned to comics and running.

Then my stepmother Edna discovered the comic books, and they were gone.

I wondered if I was going crazy. I would awaken at night, crying from a dream in which I was fleeing my stepmother. Edna would enter my room and slap me in an effort to stop the weeping, which had awakened her. By the time I figured out that the dream had merged with reality, she was gone and I would squint at the closed door, trying to separate images of light and dark.

Despite the fact that I now had Toussaint and his mother in the periphery of my life, I tried to run away.

Knowing that silence was imperative to successful flight, I took my time. It was not difficult to sneak down the staircase, my footfalls absorbed by the carpet that had through long wear become part of the risers. The front door made a sound like a cherry bomb when opened by the remote handle. I had seen Father lubricate it. I put oil in the hinges and gave the task five minutes, and the door opened with all the sound that a mouse makes when it sniffs cheese.

Golden Gate Avenue was utterly dark and surprisingly cold, the lone streetlamp at the corner of Central Avenue offering few clues and no warmth. But the street was mine, surrendered only for blinding moments as cars with overbright headlights passed.

The first time a car approached I ran from it, thinking it was an agent of Edna in hot pursuit. I could run very fast on a cold night on an empty sidewalk, my lungs bellowing as I humped arms high and hard to let my legs pump, my head vibrating synchronously with the effort as I fled my fears.

I roamed McAllister, leaning against the cold steel doors of Cutty's Garage, peering into the barred windows of the Reliance Market, missing the winos who kept guard at the Double Olive Bar, trying to recapture the now departed aromas of sizzling French fries in the General Lew Wallace Eatery. I wondered if Rupert and Dozer, the fratricidal siblings, argued after they closed the Eatery and went home to the large apartment building on Grove. Without the aromas of food, McAllister smelled sour and old. I played imaginary checkers on the linoleum grid of the barbershop floor. I projected the more complex figures of Chinese chess, *shiang chi*, onto the black-and-white squares, but could not remember all the moves for both players.

I strolled to Broderick Street, over the pavement where I had once raced when I had a home in which to hide. I looked through the iron-grate fence of Fremont Elementary, retracing beatings by Big Willie and the Bashers. I surveyed the kickball-field benches, the lunch tables, where food had been taken and little bodies stomped. I looked at that spot of the yard, knowing a truth lay in it. I looked away.

Cats chased shadowy rats on the street where Big Willie had stood on my chest. Dogs rousted garbage cans. One growled at me and I froze, waiting ten or fifteen minutes like a man who has stepped on a pressure-release-trigger land mine, until the dog had taken his pleasure with the waste. With light feet, his mangy tail down, he padded away from me and I breathed again.

This was my street, McAllister. Now, in the solace of the night, with its bullies and angry words and fists absent, I liked it. I wanted to sleep by day and to walk McAllister to the east at night. It felt safe, the biting cold welcome and fitting. For an instant, I did not want to go any farther, my feet immobilized by the vast, dark unknowns that surrounded the 'hood. I wondered if *wupo*, witches, awaited me in side alleys, or if *dufei,* bandits, were hoping to snatch the only son of the Ting clan tonight.

Ah, I thought. The *wupo* is inside the house, not here.

Feeling mildly suicidal, I crossed McAllister to Fulton, which was bold for any kid north of the park. I headed south, keeping to the shadows, crossing Grove, Hayes, and Fell, the final boundary between sanity and simple stupidity. I watched the night traffic on Fell, a big, wide thoroughfare. Where were these people going? Could I go too?

Now I was in the tall eucalyptus trees of the Panhandle itself, the glare of the streetlights swallowed in the darkness of gnarled, interwoven trees. I was in the demilitarized zone, the place of mysterious human sounds, secret passions, and dark bleeding. This was not a child's place.

I crept through the brush as only a boy with bad night vision can. Slowly, patiently, silently, over a detritus of cans, wrappers, boxes, papers. If I made a noise, I stopped. I crawled past a man and a woman whispering to each other with an intensity beyond comprehension. I shimmied up to a group of talkers sitting around a burning trash can. The fire crackled and cloaked my advance.

I listened to the men in the park. "Boogeymen" from the Haight, with deep, gravelly, bitter voices, raspy with old rumbling hungers. The humor was strained. Some of the speakers were drunk and flared at each other like the trash fire finding fuel to combust in gunfirelike consumption.

What would they do if they found me? I wondered. Nothing, I decided. They didn't care about little boys. There was little talk about sports and fighting. Someone mentioned Joe Louis, and I heard Di Maggio's name.

They were mostly concerned with women, and their meanness and beauty. The mystery of women. Those men blamed women for all their woes. Always taking things, wanting more, refusing love, yelling, complaining, comparing. I nodded my head, watching the shadowed figures gesturing, belching in hunger, nodding heads, tippling bottles.

One man held their attention as he spoke of the great Southern Pacific trains that ran from the China Basin docks to Mexico with empty freight cars, no railroad police, and a free meal at the train

stops for veterans. I was the son of a veteran. Did that count? I
didn't have a mother. Did that matter?

China Basin. It was somewhere in San Francisco, and it
sounded like China Boy, like me. It was my train. I could go to
Mexico. No Edna. No Willie and no Bashers. I would be leaving.
Could I do that?

In my mind I heard the wail of the engine calling, its
thunderous power promising fast, determined movement, high-
pumping wheels chugging tirelessly, taking me away even while I
slept in its cars.

I watched the firefly sparks of the trashy fire flicker into the
night sky, looking like the stack flames of a southbound freight,
disappearing into the swallowing blackness. For years I would
deride myself, assailing my manhood, for not taking the China
Basin train. The decision had been in my hands, but I lacked the
ability to seize an early opportunity to die a boy's lonesome death on
a distant track.

When I reached Masonic and Golden Gate, I was drawn to
Toussaint's apartment building. I climbed the outside stairs with
great stealth, thinking of his mother Mrs. LaRue, wanting a glass of
water, happy with the mere thought that she was on the other side
of the door, resting. Truly there, actually alive, to be seen and heard
again. I touched a leg. A big leg. I knew that I was dead from fright
and would be beaten afterward for clumsiness.

It was Sippy Suds, his horrendous odors mysteriously absent
in the cool of the night. He stirred slightly and began to snore
softly. He looked huge lying down, folded inside his faded, moth-
eaten, navy pea jacket. In his bent, inebriated, staggering postures
on the street, I had thought of him as short. He was actually a tall
man. His hands were pinned between his drawn-up knees. They
were huge, the fingers bent and black with the dirt of past labor. His
wrists were bony but very thick. Hands that gave precious coins
to greedy children.

His face looked as if it had been hit often by hard objects or
by an angry stepmother. It was square and hard, different colors
shading it. Bruising colors. His nose was very flat at the bridge, the

bottom of the nose turned to the side, as if an anvil had been dropped on it from an angle. The closed, trusting eyes were surrounded by scars and small mounds of built-up skin. The rough pebbles of scar tissue interrupted the deep lines that laughter had once carved into his temples.

He was a fighta, Toussaint had said.

I sat next to him, looking at him, edging closer, absorbing his kindly silent companionship, feeling safety, defeating loneliness with every moment in his company. I held my breath.

Then we breathed together, and I matched his cycle, my small puff of air emerging with his thicker cloud, both of us slowly exhaling our fatigues with bright, streetlight, vaporous breath into the foggy night. My lungs filled with soulful strength.

I wanted him to awaken and to tell me about his fights. I wanted to hear that he had won, somehow, somewhere, in his past. Together, I thought, the two of us could do anything. I sat until my bottom ached from the hardness of the stairs, and I began shivering, my thin body capsized in cold.

Bye-bye Suds, I whispered, smiling as he stirred again. I returned with small steps to the house of my stepmother, ready for neither the beginning of sleep nor the start of day.

✒ *Anne Lamott*

What my mother gave

After two nights in a row of insomnia, I finally got to bed the other night at a reasonable hour, only to be shaken awake at midnight by my 15-year-old son. My first thought was that we had an intruder, and I reached for the tennis racket I keep by my bed in case I needed to kill someone. "No, no, Mom, I just can't sleep," he cried out plaintively.

"That's terrible," I said, "to wake me, just because you can't sleep."

"But you're my mom," he said. "I'm supposed to come to you with my problems."

The first year after my mother's death, I felt a lot of sadness that I hadn't had a mother to whom I could take my problems. She was my problem, or at any rate, this is what I had always thought and continued to think. Mothers are supposed to listen and, afterward, to respond with some wisdom and perspective, but these things were not my mother's strong suit.

If you asked me, parents were supposed to affect the life of their child in such a way that the child grows up to be responsible, able to participate in life and in community. For instance, you teach a child to play so he can stay healthy, and have fun, but my mother had so pressured me to achieve at tennis that I had migraines until I quit playing tournaments. And you teach a kid to pick up after him or herself, and to make the bed in the mornings, so the kid doesn't see the mother as a servant, vibrating with martyrdom. This teaches a child that she is a part of an organism, the household, and must respect her relationship with the other inmates enough to smooth the covers, and remove any socks or juice boxes that are leaving a discernible bump. But the thing is—and I mean this nicely—my mother was kind of a slob, and I was too, until I got sober.

The fact that my mother's bed always looked like Krakatoa is actually a decent metaphor for many of the things she forgot to teach me. She made her psychic bed with a mate who felt contempt for women. Her bed was littered with wrappers and crumbs, because she did not know how to separate her pain from the great amount of food she ate, and I had to fight like mad to heal from eating disorders. She didn't know that you can take care of the inside of things—like people, or your own heart—by tending to appearances, or surfaces: You put on a little blusher or moisturizer, or you make the bed.

So because she didn't usually teach me things that helped me get through life, I didn't go to her with my problems. I went to a man, to my father. He could listen. He taught me most of life's important rules, the ones I have passed on to my son, Sam: 1) Don't act like a pig. 2) Don't cross the intersection right after the light turns green. 3) When all else fails, follow instructions. 4) Try to take a long walk every day, and keep your eyes and ears open for birds. 5) Assume that all drivers on the road are ignorant of Rules 1 and 2, or that they drive like Nana Miller.

The second year after my mother died, my child became a teenager. I knew by then that adolescents are always trying to shred your respect—that's their job. They are trying to individuate, which seemed natural when I was doing it with my mother, but which is wrenching now. There was a huge difference, though, in my mother's house when she was raising teenagers. In my house, not everything becomes a pitched battle.

For 35 years now, since I was 16 and *Ms.* Magazine first came out, other girls and women have been telling me their deepest secrets and truths, and we have been laughing ourselves sick—or rather well—over this stuff. I learned that women could stand up to anyone, and that it was OK to be angry, and that, in fact, if you were over 13 and had been raised in America and were not furious, there was something wrong. So I had gotten to be really angry along the way, but my mother hadn't gotten to be. She stuffed it, she ate at it, and it ate at her and ultimately made her crazy. As a child, I was dependent on someone who was always on the verge of implosion.

I was able to scatter her ashes during the second year after her death, was able to cry and to feel a huge sadness, for both of us. I ached for her, for all that had been so impossible for her to bear, for the bad cards she had been dealt. But I was still fighting for my life, about to turn 50 and still trying to learn the things she forgot to teach me—that I was beautiful, that I had to tell the truth, even with men and business associates, that what I saw and sensed was pretty reliable. I saw her as the foil, believing that I had grown to be a lovable, strong and sometimes wild person because I had had to resist her so ferociously.

I didn't write about my mother much in the third year after she died. I was still trying to get my argument straight: When her friends or our relatives wondered why I was still so hard on her, I could really lay out the case for what it had been like to be raised by someone who had loathed herself, her husband, even her own name. (She went by Nikki, which was the name of a girl on the radio in Liverpool when she was little.) Anyone could see why I had such a hard time with her, and what an infinitely good daughter I had been to take such good care of her anyway, her entire life—well, except during the worst years of my adolescence.

However , this left me without a mother, except for the mother of jokes and reminiscences with people to whom she had been close. Except for the mother I could do a dead-on impersonation of, with her imperial madness, her royal kindness, the poise marbled into all her self-loathing and struggles. I could even reminisce with my boyfriend, who never met her, because he had the same sort of queenly English mother—with the same throat and nostrils, the same glacial kindliness, the same skittering, demanding qualities, the airs, and the high color.

But now in the fourth year of her death, I can see in my son's eyes so many things I was missing before. My mother's eyes were large and brown, like my son's, but unlike Sam's, they were always frantic, like a hummingbird who can't quite find the flower but keeps jabbing around. I can see in Sam's what an embarrassment I am sometimes, with my hippie clothes, my anxieties, my many mistakes. I can see that he understands, at a much earlier age than I did—again, because his mother was raised with women's liberation—that we are all doing the best we can, and that some days go better than others. I can see how much Sam does for other people. I can see his deep sensitivity, beneath the annoyance of having to live with him on bad days. I see us explode, and apologize, and that is his redemption, over and over again.

I see that children fill the existential hollowness many people feel; that when we have children, we know they will need us, and maybe love us, but we don't have a clue how hard it is going to be. We can't understand when we're pregnant, or when our siblings are expecting, how profound it is to have a shared history with a younger generation: blood, genes, humor. It means we were actually here, on Earth, for a time—like the Egyptians with their pyramids, only with children. It's a great experiment to wait and see what will come of it. With buildings, the result is often fantastic, but with people, the result is almost always a bit of a mess.

And that is what my mother has given me in the fourth year of her death. I can see with my spirit's eyes that out of that mess came a bunch of gifts—of generosity in the midst of being broke, of survival and, most of all, of having a gift for friendships. These are what my mother had in spades, and what I have, too. This is what our family and friends remember—how she always bailed people out and helped people not feel poor, even if that meant going into debt herself. How so many women of her generation were wiped out by the whacking down that life gave them, but how my mother stayed one step ahead of the abyss with a series of Monsieur Hulot-like lurches and sidesteps, until finally, the plague of Alzheimer's filled her brain.

The other day, I found a description of something I'd written the summer before she died, when she started calling me to tell me she was getting us the great box, with cheese! It was going to be so wonderful. "What box, Mom?" I kept asking, and she'd get furious with herself and then with me. And she'd call the next day to say she had gotten us the box.

"It's not a box containing cheese?" I asked, thinking of Pepperidge Farm crackers.

"Oh, for Christ's sake," she snapped, and hung up.

I went down to her apartment the next day, and when she opened the door, she said, "The man brought the box!"

I stepped inside to see, and there on her television set was a cable box that she'd rented so she and I could watch Wimbledon together on pay-per-view. Then she flung open the refrigerator door to show me all the cheese

---

Typical Blane and Sean, Blane's sixteenth birthday, June, 1986. I left for NOLS a few days later.

❧ *Sean Wilsey*

Excess

In the beginning we were happy. And we were always excessive. So in the beginning we were happy to excess.

We were Mom and Dad and I—three palindromes!—and we lived eight hundred feet in the air above San Francisco; an apartment at the top of a building at the top of a hill: full of light, full of voices, full of windows, full of water and bridges and hills.

Mom was the center. Mom was irresistible. Whatever she was saying or wearing or smelling of was captivating—all our senses were attuned to her. As soon as I was old enough to walk I tried on her shoes and evening gowns and perfume, admired and wanted to be like her, so much that they had me seeing a shrink by the time I was three. The shrink said I needed to spend more time with my dad. But how? Mom was irresistible.

Mom was a writer. Most days she was at her desk, on the phone, with a yellow legal pad in front of her. Mom wrote books, and a column for the San Francisco *Examiner*. I came to see her first thing when I got home from school. My mom the author! I thought. When she saw me she smiled, waved and mouthed the word "Tab." I reversed the maneuver 99.9 percent of my gender performed upon seeing her and went away, back down the long upstairs hall, to the bar off the den. I opened a cabinet, removed a cut crystal goblet, set it down on the Formica counter with both hands—*Bng*—and filled it with ice-maker ice. Then I took a Tab from the bar's minirefrigerator, poured, and carried it back down the long hall. The ice clinked as I walked. The clinks were like music, like happiness; I jostled the Tab for joy, made it sizzle up out of the goblet at me like a miniature stadium full of applause.

Mom had published two books—one about throwing parties, one about battling malevolent ghosts—and was working on a third, about her childhood in Texas and Oklahoma.

As far as I could tell Dad's job was to please Mom. He was solicitous and full of care. He gave Mom everything she wanted. He helped her want things she did not know to want.

Early every morning, Mom, Dad and I took walks around Russian Hill in matching blue jumpsuits with white piping, *Royal Tenenbaums*—style.

One Sunday, on a shrink-mandated father-and-son outing, Dad took me across the bay on the ferry, re-creating the commute he made as a boy, before the Golden Gate Bridge was completed, from Catholic school in San Francisco to his home in Marin. Halfway there it started to rain, and we didn't have any umbrellas, so when we arrived we stood in a doorway near the water.

Dad hadn't shaved since Friday morning before work, and he looked rough. Even I could see it. Our matching jumpsuits were sad without Mom. Dad lit a cigarette. We looked out at the water.

A man with a box and an umbrella strode past, glanced at us, stopped fifty feet on, turned, walked back, and handed the box to Dad.

"I can't give you anything else," he said. "But take this."

Dad said, "Thank you," and took the box.

The man looked at me, looked at the ground, walked away.

Dad smoked till the man was out of sight, then he threw his cigarette in the gutter and opened the box.

"He gave us donuts!" I shouted.

Dad looked at me and started chuckling. "That guy thinks we don't have any money." He took a donut, laughed again, and blew powdered sugar out of his mouth.

I ate a glazed, and then a chocolate with sprinkles. Dad ate all the rest, steadily, devouring them with great relish and no preference for jelly over old-fashioned over chocolate or bear claw—only pleasure, and great amusement.

At home I was either left alone, or overwhelmed with attention. Mom and Dad were either oblivious or hyperaware. They disappeared on a trip for seventeen days and left me with the maid. On Mom's return I ignored her when she called my name. She had my ears examined. They were infected. I needed surgery; tubes installed to drain them. I was four. Mom set herself the task of increasing my medical vocabulary, to make the hospital less frightening. (When an orderly rolled me into the operating room I asked him, "Are you the anesthesiologist?") I received books to read during my recovery, and became the kind of kid who spends all his time alone, reading, till Mom noticed my left eye didn't turn all the way to the left; then it was back to the doctor.

I had a friend down the hall, in the long shadow of our building, whose mother cooked us meatloaf. When I discovered meatloaf, and that other mothers regularly cooked it for their children, I went home and said, "Other mothers cook. Why don't you cook?"

Without hesitation Mom said, "Other mothers don't write books."

It was the end of that question for me. And thenceforth, as if
to compensate for not cooking the food we were eating, she began
reading from her books at the dinner table.

Mom was a captivating reader. She'd won the all-state
elocution award in Oklahoma, in the forties, and when she told a
story, especially a story about her childhood, Mom made me love
words.

But Mom had lots of other people to captivate. The apartment
was headquarters for a salon-*cum*-luncheon--called the Roundtable—
where Mom hosted *conversation*. The guests were notorious
strangers. They always came, if for no other reason than to see
the view. They were: union leaders; unionized prostitutes; Alex
Haley; Native American secessionists; Agnes Moorehead; radical
lesbians; Nobel laureates; Joan Baez; Black Panthers; Dear Abby;
an astronaut; Eldridge Cleaver; Jessica Mitford; Gloria Steinem; a
Catholic priest; a woman who had murdered her husband; Shirley
Temple; a lesbian priest; Betty Friedan; welfare mothers; Werner
Erhard; a Soviet ballerina; Daniel Ellsberg. And so on.

Jessica Mitford was an old British woman with huge round
glasses who proclaimed, "When I die I've given instructions that I
want to be buried like this," and then pulled one corner of her mouth
up and dragged the other one down and eyed the other guests (the
mayor, a plastic surgeon, Agnes Moorehead, Shirley Temple.) "I
want to make sure you all check on it. That's the way I want to
look." Eldridge Cleaver brought Dad velvet flower-embroidered
shorts that had a codpiece hanging down the front. Once I came
home from school and no one was in the kitchen. The cook and the
housekeeper—in French maid's uniforms—had joined the table for
lunch with Betty Friedan and Gloria Steinem. (Said Mom, "They
were the perfect people to talk with domestic workers about the
difficulty of working in someone else's home.")

Mom presided over the Roundtable with a silver bell that she
rang to get everyone's attention. After ringing the bell Mom directed
the conversation by asking questions. And as I went about my only-
child activities—searching out a wire strippers to connect a camera

battery to a nail and make a laser gun; constructing an orange juice dispenser out of Dad's discarded WaterPik dental hygiene machine (So I could have breakfast in my room); synthesizing an alcohol-free imitation wine; using bendable drink straws to siphon and circulate cold water throughout my bathroom during a heat wave—words found their way into my newly-drained ears:

MOM: You were once behind walls, weren't you? In a concentration camp?

WOMAN'S VOICE: I was a refugee. My country is Yugoslavia, and we are the troublemakers of the world, you know.

DAD: Just you?

WOMAN'S VOICE: In 1941, when the Germans took over, these invaders, the Germans and Croats, caught a million Serbs and killed them overnight and sent them down to the river. It's not something to talk about at lunchtime,.

MOM: We talk about everything at lunchtime here!

The battery heated the nail until it turned bright orange!

MOM: How do you feel you have changed?

MAN'S VOICE: I was a Marxist. I had rejected spiritual values. But then…I saw the design in nature and I was convinced there was a Creator…It was a bad time for me. I wanted to go home to the United States. Friends of mine got into power and I thought they would help me but they didn't. The whole bottom of my world fell out. I went into a deep depression. I felt trapped. I had a wife and two children and my children didn't even speak English. They were going to French schools and becoming little Frenchie fried people. One night on my balcony I just caved in. This is down near Cannes on the Mediterranean coast. A lot of people ask me, like, were you drunk, had you been smoking? I was not high on anything. I was looking at the moon, a full moon. I had been thinking of killing myself. I had the pistol. And I wondered if what I was seeing was a sign that death was near. And then my image fell away and on the moon I saw a procession of my heroes: Fidel Castro, Mao Tse-tung, Karl Marx, Friedrich Engels. And then the image of

Jesus Christ. That was an unwelcome image because I didn't have
anything to do with him. It was like the last straw. I started crying.
Just gushing out, real violent. I was trembling and I had the sense
that my soul was trembling. I was down on my knees hanging onto
the rail. And then I ran inside for a Bible. And it was there, this
book I never read. I found the Twenty-third Psalm, which I had
learned as a child. But I didn't know where to find the Lord's Prayer.
That's what happened, O.K.

The WaterPik fired orange juice across the room!

MOM: Has winning the Nobel Prize been helpful in your work?

WOMAN'S VOICE: Oh, yes!

I put the synthetic wine in a wine bottle. Dad drank it with
dinner and couldn't tell the difference!
WOMAN'S VOICE: What propels you to get rich?
DAD: (In a voice that suggested maybe he was putting
everyone on, or maybe he was completely serious): Greed.

My bathroom got cooler and I ran downstairs shouting, "Mom,
Dad—finally one of my inventions works!"
    . . .

Mom loved her luncheons. Mom loved emotions. "All these
strangers, they sobbed like babies," she told me recently. "And they
became my dear, dear friends." The apartment was an accelerator for
emotions, a controlled environment where they could be witnessed
without effect. Neutralized and admired. We were eight hundred
feet above it all. Little did I—who had known only happiness or
loneliness—know the variety emotion could provide. That pain
moved in mysterious ways. That it could fly, swim, tunnel; was
amphibious, ambidextrous, aerodynamic; a breeze and a smothering

blanket and a storm. That emotions would knock our tower down to the ground and none of these strangers would help us.

When I was five Mom and Dad rented a house in the Napa Valley, and Dad befriended a man called Frenchie Meyers who wore suspenders and owned a junk yard nearby—fifty acres covered in thirty-foot heaps of smashed cars, flat-tired trailers full of old glass doorknobs, two aircraft hangars (one stuffed full of forklifts, tractors, and power tools and guarded by Sam, a glass-blue-eyed wolf dog, the other converted into a machine shop and guarded by an anvil of a bulldog named Jezebel). Dad let me play in an old school bus parked beneath an ancient willow tree. How old? Centuries old, Dad informed me. I played for hours beneath that green canopy, in that yellow bus, while Dad talked to Frenchie.

Dad made Frenchie an offer to buy it all, said Frenchie could keep on living in his little house on the edge of the junk, rent-free forever. Frenchie accepted.

Dad built a hill—flood protection---and Mom's dream house on the hill. Mom landscaped the junk into trees and lawns and an hourglass-shaped carp pond. The school bus got towed. I built a tree house in the willow. I tried to construct a car out of Frenchie's leftover junk. On the weekends, Dad wore a JC Penney work shirt and led a crew of men planting grass, grapes and flowers, and shoring up the eroding banks of the Napa River, which ran along the property's edge.

Perfect happiness started flowing. Mom brought Dad cooling beverages while he worked. We had picnics. I made friends with a Mexican kid down the road, and we hammered nails into the tree house. At night Dad showed us World War I movies on an old projector. Mom's best friend, Dede Traina (pronounced Try-een-nah), had a place nearby, and she was over all the time. Hundreds of people came to our housewarming party, where a Catholic priest blessed the premises and Benny Goodman played live. This party blended into another and another. The biggest was a *Gone with the Wind* ball, when Dede upstaged everyone by wearing Scarlett O'Hara's green-and-white hoop dress from the movie, refabricated by the original designer; it was like the willow tree, and I crawled underneath, following her sons, Todd and Trevor. There was a whole world under there!

Mom said, "Sean, get out!"

Dede said, "No, he can stay."

I wanted to spend my whole life there.

Mom's previous best friend had died in a mysterious fire while living in Mom's old apartment, shortly after my parents were married. Dede Traina arrived in Mom's life in the early seventies (around the same time my shrink told Mom to stop spending so much time with me). Dede was new to San Francisco, fifteen years younger than Mom, in her early thirties, unhappily married. Mom liked Dede. Dad liked that Dede came from an old East Coast family. Dede was grateful; every time she visited our house she brought gifts. Once it was a coffee-table book of "history's great beauties."

She climbed up on Mom's bed and they looked at it together. Helen of Troy, Marilyn Monroe, Jackie O.

"You're one of them, Pat," Dede said.

"Oh, Dede, you are making my day," Mom said, beaming.

Before long Dede was the first person Mom would call in the morning, and the last she'd talk to at the end of the day.

One time, when my parents were out, Dede appeared in my doorway.

"Come with me, Sean," she said. "I've got a surprise for you."

I wondered how she had gotten into our house. But it didn't matter. She was Mom's best friend. I went downstairs, got in her car, and we drove to the supermarket. She took me to the candy aisle.

"Let's pretend it's Halloween," Dede said. "And we can have as much candy as we want."

I was tentative. Yeah? Was this possible?

Dede started grabbing bags off the shelves, opening them, and handing me Reese's Peanut Butter Cups and mini Hershey bars. She was like a kid with the power of an adult. She told me I could eat them right there in the aisles, demonstrated, and nobody stopped her. It was as though she owned the store. Maybe she did own the store! I started eating. We filled a cart with candy. I was flying on sugar. In the checkout line I chewed a Starburst and drank a Coke. Dede drank a Pepsi Lite and ate hunks of something called almond roca.

"This is my very favorite candy," she whispered. Then she gave me a bite, holding a piece and placing it on my tongue. It was chocolate-covered toffee, studded with little filings of some exotic nut—sophisticated and delicious. *Wow*.

We mostly saw Dede and her boys, and sometimes her husband, John, for picnics and bike rides and lunches in the country. Mom had started a bicycling club that took back roads through the valley every weekend. Dede and John and Todd and Trevor always rode elegant European-style bicycles called Univegas, while Mom and Dad and I rode Huffys. Dede's elegant bike was frequently breaking down, but my dad would stop and help her.

In San Francisco Dede and John Traina lived in Pacific Heights, a neighborhood of mansions not far from Russian Hill but stodgy by comparison. During the week she came over to our house by herself. Dede became a member of the family, part my big sister, part Mom's little sister, part something else.

Dede was kooky, like family, too.

One day after lunch, she told mom and Dad and me how full she was and asked, "Do you want to see how I get into my really tight jeans? I have to lie down, like this." "She lay down, unzipped—pink underwear stood out against the Kelly green of her jeans---"and then wriggle in." She pulled the waist down to demonstrate, and then started yanking it back up as she swiveled her hips side to side on the carpet.

Very difficult, I thought.

When I was nine I asked Dad about sex. He drove me to the Fairmont Hotel, on nearby Nob Hill, parked across the street in a loading zone, and told me to wait in the car.

Then he crossed the semicircular drive of the hotel, held the
door for a woman, exchanged a pleasnt word, smiled (lips closed
to hide his stained teeth), and disappeared into the building. I
looked around Nob Hill: gray Grace Cathedral (where I'd be going
to school soon); red-brick Pacific Union Club (an institution Dad
reviled—though later joined—because "somebody blackballed me
for being married to a Jewish woman," which required a complicated
explanation of blackballing and Judaism, forever twinning the two in
my mind); shreds of blue bay between old brownstone skyscrapers;
green geometric Huntington Park where Thuy, a Vietnamese
"governess" (to use Mom's word) whom I'd asked to marry me
the year before, stealing a ring from her so I could give it back as a
wedding present, once snatched up a pigeon and held it to her breast
while she told me her brother had been killed by the Viet Cong.

Dad came out of the Fairmont holding a *Playboy*. He carried it
in plain sight. I could make it out from across the street. I watched in
awe—a small, beautiful, inadequately clothed woman, arriving with
Dad. He got in and handed it to me.

"Here," he said. "We'll look at some women's bodies."

The cover woman looked at me liked she *loved me. I loved
her!*

Dad opened the magazine to the table of contents.

"What should we look at first?" he asked.

"The lady on the cover," I said in a very quiet voice. It seemed
faithless to look at anybody else.

Dad laughed, not unkindly, and said, "Well, there's a lot more
in here. Let's look at the centerfold."

My vocabulary was getting ever larger.

He unfolded and I stared. The centerfold was the most
beautiful picture of the most beautiful woman in the world that
month. After a couple of minutes he said, "The centerfold doesn't
have to be your favorite. It could be anyone." He handed me the
magazine. I leafed through. Breasts. Lace. A completely naked
woman in a body stocking—a totally confusing garment. I stopped
at a half-page picture of a woman with straight dark hair reclining
on a rubber-latticed pool chaise, a gold unicorn pendant on a

thin gold chain around her neck, and dangling down between her breasts, which were tanned, dewy, and a bit smaller—more modest, I thought—than the other breasts in the magazine. The unicorn stopped me. It was an amulet of power. Like the magic ring in my favorite book, *The Hobbit*. She was beautiful and mysterious and wise and possibly part elvish.

Dad turned back to the centerfold. I had a confusing erection. The centerfold was beautiful. She was tall and blonde and proud, standing completely straight, completely naked, and facing the camera. I had only ever desired toys, and now I desired her. She was motivating me. I felt like doing her bidding. I wasn't sure what she was bidding me to do. Grab the magazine to my chest? Crinkle the pages as hard as I could. Eat them? Roll around in the backseat with them. Beat someone in wrestling? (I was one of the better wrestlers in my Catholic grade school.) Everything hurt. I had hot magma flowing through my head and arms.

Dad started the car and we drove home, me holding the *Playboy*. In the building's garage he took it back and said, "I'll keep this, but whenever you need it come ask me. We can look at it some more, together. But you can't keep it."

After we'd both looked at the issue a few times, another month came, and the overhill ride to the Fairmont happened again. It became a father-son tradition.

After a few months, Dad told me, "I'm going to keep these in a drawer from now on, and you can come take them any time you want. You don't have to ask me. But you have to put them back when you're done looking at them. I'll be checking on that."

My parents' third home was a restaurant halfway down Nob Hill, toward the seedy Tenderloin—run-down on the outside, clubby and leathery and lustrous on the inside. I was a nonspilling, silent-when-told-to-be child, so, also when I was nine, my parents convinced the management to make an exception to their unbendable no-children rule, and for nearly a year I almost lived there, too. It was like traveling overseas to a ruleless country. All proscriptions were thrown out. I got to stay up late. I was an adult. The maitre d' told us what a great table he had for us, down the hall, past the cigar lady in her closet—who waved at me as if from a ship—past the bathrooms with their zebra-skin doors, in the dim, glowing hum of the main room, called the Captain's Cabin, which grew louder as we entered, as if we were newspaper thrown on a fire.

A waiter came, took Dad's drink order—"Tanqueray gin on the rocks"—and quickly came back. The air around Dad started to smell like fuel.

Mom ordered. Dad ordered. They ordered for me: an elevated silver platter of spare ribs with a candle underneath, accompanied by a butterfly-shaped dish, one wing full of hot yellow mustard, the other sweet red sauce. Dad looked deeply content. Mom smiled her radiant, irresistible-to-photographers smile. People came to say hello.

Dad drank his flammable Tanqueray gin on the rocks, slowly, and leaned back into the banquette, above which maxims were set into wooden plaques with chiseled Gothic letters. Above him it said:

> *No chord of music has yet been found*
> *To even equal that sweet sound*
> *Which to my mind all else surpasses*
> *The clink of ice in crystal glasses*

I knew about the clink of ice in crystal glasses: it was a sound that meant all was well, everything was in it place, no mistakes were being made, everybody loved each other. I looked at the maxim on the plaque above Mom and Dad and I knew we were doing everything perfectly, and as long as the crystal and ice kept clinking there was nothing to worry about.

Mom and Dad got divorced that same year—after ten years without once fighting, and regular reassurances that they would never get divorced—and when they did it was vicious and corrosive and melodramatic and strange, like having all your clothes taken away, being forced to the end of a narrow hallway, and having a flaming car battery hurled at you.

I thought their marriage was perfect until one night in the middle of dinner. This was the second night in a row that Mom had placed her head in her hands and started crying at the table while Dad carried on making conversation as though nothing were out of the ordinary. I said, "Dad, what's the matter with Mom?" He hesitated and she blurted out miserably, "Something terrible has happened." Dad looked unreadable. I realized that this was serious. Dad said, "We're going to tell you about it after dinner." I tried to prepare myself. I tried to think of the worst thing that could ever happen happening.

I said, "Has Dede died?"

Mom and Dad told me that Dad would be moving out. A few days later I went and spent the night with him in the Fairmont Hotel, and for the first time he told me the following, which he would repeat many times over the years: "If your mother had cared as much about being a wife as she did about being a star, we'd still be married."

✎ *Lincoln Mitchell*

The Pizza Guy

Among the emails, phone calls and notes congratulating us after my younger son, Reuben, was born was one from one of my oldest friends from San Francisco, asking if I had named him "after the pizza guy." Reuben was named after my wife's grandmother Ruth. But after he was born, and as we began to call him Ruby, I found myself thinking more about "the pizza guy."

"The pizza guy" was Danny Rubinstein, known as Ruby. I had worked for him for one summer, at his restaurant Ruby's Gourmet Pizza, fifteen years before Reuben was born. Ruby's Gourmet Pizza was one of San Francisco's—and perhaps America's—first restaurants that sold pizza made from gourmet ingredients. A not-particularly large slice piece of pizza at Ruby's ranged from $2.35 to

$3.25, a lot of money for a piece slice in 1986—even one with sun-dried tomatoes, smoked salmon, pesto, or escargot.

I was well into my thirties before I had a job I enjoyed quite so much. The other folks who worked at Ruby's were an eclectic San Francisco group: the new age waitress; Ruby's uptight and nebbishy partner; the nutty stoner cook who believed the world could be explained through astrology; the weirdly quiet delivery guy who believed he was on the verge of a patent which was going to make him a millionaire; the tough but friendly waitress; and the two cooks from Minnesota who were old friends from the Navy. I played the role of the hippie college student who liked to talk politics and baseball, and flirt with the waitresses and customers.

Ruby, a 60's era hippie in his mid-thirties, presided over this scene. He was one of those people who came to San Francisco on a brief visit and never left. Ruby had protested the Vietnam War and gone to Columbia University on a football scholarship before coming to San Francisco, like thousands of others of his generation. I never knew why he came; perhaps he was following some hippie dream, or came to be with a woman. But by the time I met him more than a decade later, San Francisco was his home. During the 1970s, he had bounced from job to job, driven a cab, waited tables, and begun to develop a passion for cooking. San Francisco was a different place then, where a single man would work odd jobs and still afford a nice place with some friends in a funky neighborhood.

I didn't realize it at the time—because San Francisco was all I had known—but Ruby's Pizza and Ruby himself captured much of what had made San Francisco a special place to grow up. It was the last time I would really feel it, because I was changing, and more importantly, so was the city in which I had lived since I was three years old.

Growing up in San Francisco meant being a child in a city that for many was the symbol of the promise and hope of the 1960s and 1970s. Nobody wrote song lyrics in the 1960s advising "If you're going to Columbus, Ohio be sure to wear some flowers in your hair," or urging people to "save up all your bread and fly Trans Love Airways to Kenosha, Wisconsin." Some of those who came to San

Francisco became bit players in childhoods like mine. While our parents did est, got divorced, tried to find themselves, and enjoyed their new lives and freedoms, we attended Catholic school, did our homework, and played sports on the streets.

Of course, not all of us came from that world. Some of my friends and the kids I knew growing up were the sons and daughters of what had once been San Francisco's huge white and Asian working class, or its wealthy elite. Their parents, unlike mine, embraced the San Francisco of the 1970s with far less enthusiasm. They saw their city changing dramatically and being taken over by outsiders.

This difference was never made more clear to me than on that Monday in late November of 1978. Upon returning from lunch to my sixth grade science class, the nun who taught us announced that Mayor Moscone and Supervisor Harvey Milk had been assassinated. Some of us were stunned. In my household, Milk had been well-liked because he had been a fellow progressive Jew from New York. In the homes of many of my classmates, he was a symbol of the unwelcome changes to their San Francisco. There were more than a few cheers and celebratory shouts of "they killed that fag." My mother's friends, most of whom were recent migrants to San Francisco, were mostly shocked and outraged by the assassinations.

But many of my Catholic School classmates argued that Milk and Moscone's assassin, former Supervisor Dan White, deserved a light sentence because he had lived an exemplary life and only made one mistake. By 1986, changes in the economy—along with events like those of November 1978—had altered San Francisco. It was a much tougher and less welcoming place for people like Ruby. Those 1970s migrants who were still driving cabs ands waiting on tables were beginning to struggle.

More gray was beginning to be visible in their beards and curls, and their tie-dyed T-shirts and peasant blouses were beginning to fray. Many went back home; others cut their hair and sought better paying jobs in San Francisco or elsewhere. Some struggled to find a way to live in the new San Francisco while remaining true to the vision that had originally brought them there.

My San Francisco seemed divided between the working class families who had been there for generations, and those who had come to San Francisco in the 1960s and 1970s—including Jesuit dropouts, radical ministers, many different kinds of transplanted New Yorkers, single mothers starting over, filmmakers, and even the occasional conventional married couple. It was giving way to a city of a new generation of hipster migrants, immigrants from Asia and Central America, and a boom-and-bust cycle of economic growth.

For a few years, Ruby sought to make room for himself in the new San Francisco by seeking to invent himself as a 1980-s entrepreneur. It was a tough transition for Ruby, whose sensibilities, lifestyle, and politics hadn't changed since he had protested the war at Columbia.

On the surface, Ruby seemed to be able to pull it off. He was not one of those arrogant Reagan-era yuppies who talked about finance, wore a suit, voted Republican, lived in the Marina district and yes, paid eighteen dollars for an escargot pizza from Ruby's Gourmet Pizza. Ruby seemed to retain much of the style and attitudes of his youth. That someone could live that way was something of a revelation to me. I viewed many adults Ruby's age with whom I came into contact as either yuppies or aging hippies.

Towards the former group I felt a nasty adolescent contempt. My feelings toward the latter group were more generous, but I knew that I wanted more for myself when I was that age. As a successful Jewish hippie-turned entrepreneur who still wore longish hair and a beard, dressed mostly in jeans and t-shirts, found time to attend the odd Grateful Dead show, and surrounded himself with beautiful and hip women, Ruby was a role model for me. I admired how he seemed to be able to run a successful business while still finding time for what then seemed like the most important things in life.. He was the first adult whose life I could have imagined having for myself and I think he saw me as something of a younger version of himself.

Ruby and I spent many mornings together chopping vegetables and herbs for the busy dinner hour while discussing baseball, women, politics, music, and life. If business was very slow, we would sit in the backyard, drink a beer, and enjoy the fresh air.

As we sat there under the only-sometimes warm San Francisco sun, Ruby would fall into a playful tone. What had once been a Midwestern accent had given way to the expressions and accents of his adopted hometown, but the occasional Yiddish inflections and vocabulary remained.

After a big evening when the restaurant did a lot of business, Ruby would occasionally send me on my way with a bottle of wine or a six pack of beer—his way of expressing gratitude.

I enjoyed Ruby too much to raise the questions which now seem so obvious to me. How come I never knew his real name until the morning his mother called asking for "Danny"? Although he was flirtatious and charming with all the women who wandered into the restaurant, why didn't he seem to have a girlfriend or even more than a few dates with any one woman that summer? Why had he spent more than a decade bouncing from job to job? When he talked about his past, it was always on his terms. He never really responded to my questions so much as he riffed about what was on his mind on any particular day. But if you grew up in San Francisco in the 1970s, you were used to people that age being vague about their pasts, alluding only occasionally to hometowns, careers, marriages, divorces, and life before coming to San Francisco. On some level I knew there was more to Ruby than met the eye, but I was enjoying the job too much and was taken in by his charisma and energy.

People like Ruby had formed the background of my childhood, but before that summer, that is where they had remained. For me, Ruby became the stand-in for that entire generation of migrants to San Francisco. He was a thirty-five-year-old man with great stories to tell who was still able to charm almost anybody, but who, while presenting himself as a successful entrepreneur, was struggling to make his business work, had a murky past, had no family or financial security, and still shared a flat in Noe Valley with a roommate.

A chapter in my life closed when I walked out of Ruby's Pizza as an employee for the last time. The summer of 1986 was not the end of my youth, nor was it my last summer in San Francisco, but it was close to being both. In addition to the hours I spent at Ruby's Pizza, I filled my time hanging out at Baker Beach and Golden Gate

Park with my old friends from school, spending my tip money at San Francisco's amazing array of ethnic restaurants, cruising around the city in my used Honda Civic, sleeping with a beautiful woman from my old high school who had wandered into Ruby's for lunch early that summer, and spending the few hours when I wasn't either working or seeing old friends, at cafes and used book stores on Clement street.

I began thinking of Ruby the pizza guy again when another Ruby came into my life. I occasionally told my son about the pizza guy for who, at least in his father's eyes, Reuben had been partially named. I had told my son I would someday take him to meet the other Ruby, but somehow it always fell through the cracks. In preparation for a trip to San Francisco, I googled "Danny Rubinstein" and "pizza". A link appeared to an article. I was shocked as I read through it. Danny Rubinstein, my friend and erstwhile role model, had jumped off of the Golden Gate Bridge on August 2, 2004.

When I read that article, I felt light-headed and sick to my stomach.

Typing the previous paragraph makes me feel the same way. The article mentioned the Ruby I remembered—the entrepreneur and chef, the football scholarship to Columbia, the childhood in Chicago—but it also told a much darker and sadder story of a Ruby I had not known. Ruby's life had been one of struggle against depression and other psychological conditions which had caused him great suffering and destroyed his relationships, friendships, and business. I had not known, or even really suspected any of this. When Ruby jumped off the Golden Gate Bridge—that prototypically and almost romantic San Francisco way to commit suicide—he was a fifty-two-year-old unemployed man, taking borrowed anti-depressants in an effort to defeat the demons that were finally overtaking him. I realized that I had known Ruby for a brief moment in his life when everything was going right for him, when it looked like he might just be able to make it in the new San Francisco. His business was growing and turning a good profit. He was surrounded by friends and co-workers who liked and respected him.

The article described Ruby pulling his used Ford Explorer into a parking space near the bridge, walking out over the water, and jumping. I have tried to visualize Ruby's last minutes and cannot. It's probably better that way. When I think of Ruby, I want to remember his smiling face as he made pizza, showing off the new Saab he had purchased with the money from his successful business, his sense of humor, and the friendship he showed towards a young college student trying to figure things out in life.

It saddens me that the two Rubys will never meet, and that Ruby the Pizza guy will never know how much he really meant to the young kid who delivered pizza for him in the summer of 1986.

"Ruby the Pizza Guy" by Lincoln Mitchell from *Instant City Issue 6. The Haight, The Marina & Fisherman's Wharf copyright* © Lincoln Mitchell. Reprinted by permission. Photo anof Lincoln Mitchell and his brother reprinted by permission of Lincoln Mitchell.

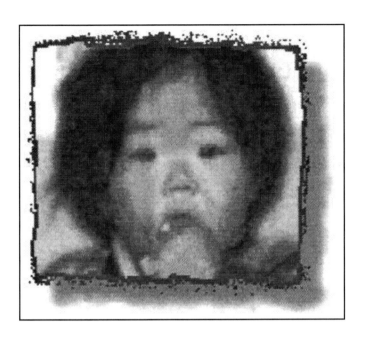

❧ *Margaret Cho*

Bravery

I have always thought of myself as brave. I have also always thought there would be people, boys especially, who would admire me, look at me, fawn over me. And there were—until I was eight and did two terrible, unforgivable things in the third grade. They happened within a period of two weeks. The first was during a bell rehearsal for the Christmas program. We were all handed very expensive, delicate, rare brass bells with which to play "Greensleeves" and we were warned and warned again and threatened and warned some more about the value of the bells. We were made to wear cotton gloves so that we would not get our fingerprints on the precious fucking bells. As I was putting my gloves on, bell stuck between my upper arm and my side, I dropped the bell and it shattered on the ground. It was an E flat or

C sharp or something definitely irreplaceable, so when the choir sang "What child is this…" the word child came without a musical accompaniment, naked, the brutal reminder to me and to all the rest of Grade Three of my grievous act.

Some time later, the worse of the two incidents occurred. During another bell rehearsal, as I had no bell to play, I sat in the back of class fidgeting and counting my fingers or something. I really had to pee, so I went to the front of the class and said to the teacher, "I have to pee." And she said, "Just wait." I returned to the back of class and the business of idling, when I was hit with an urgent, desperate need to pee that would not wait. I had to do it. After the rehearsal, half-midget perennial spinster Miss Cinnamon said, "Okay, you can go now." I answered, quite wittily I must say, "I already did."

I think that I was so used to horror, my little life had already endured such atrocities, that I was unfazed by my "accident." I sat there in thoroughly wet, itchy pants with a pool of urine underneath me, cultivating a "been there, done that" attitude. This highly disturbed the teachers, and when they asked if I wanted to go home and change, if I wanted my mom to come and get me, if there was someone they could call—I looked down at my pee-splattered Buster Browns and said, "No. Why would you want to do that?" and went off to play kickball. And I thought nobody had wanted me on their team before.

The taunts and the teasing came later. At this point, I think everyone was too afraid of me to make fun of me. They treated me like Damien in *The Omen*, as if one look of my evil eye would render them incontinent. The spell was broken soon enough. I was the pariah of the schoolyard, shunned as if I had the floor-length beard and long curly nails of the unwashed untouchables of India. To me, "recess" meant "riot," the time of day I stood between massive groups of eight-year-olds fighting over whether I could be called the Bell Breaker or the Pee Girl. I was stoic, silent, nonviolent even back then. I didn't pay attention.. But I stayed at that same school for five more years, which is forever when you are a kid, and I must

admit, it *wore me down*. I think I lost something there—an interior
brightness. The luster and the silver lining and the Tootsie Roll
center and the brave one in me went far underground, now surfacing,
twisted, perverted, deformed, with a dowager's hump and a bad
nervous tic, but tougher still.

My family went to church every Sunday, at first to the one
by Stonestown, where my grandfather led the services, and later to
the big Korean Methodist Church on Powell Street that was in the
middle of Chinatown. Sometimes big Chinese funeral processions
would lurch slowly down the street. There would be a brass band
made up of men dressed like they were in the military, playing
solemnly as they marched by. Then there'd be a black convertible,
with an enormous black-and white photo of the deceased, bordered
with black bands to signify the departure into the afterlife, attached
to the windshield. The hearse would follow, its windows crammed
with flowers behind a white curtain, hiding the mysterious gleaming
casket. I wanted to hold my breath as it went by. I thought if I got
too close and looked into the hearse, a bony hand would emerge from
it and drag me inside. Carloads of mourners trailed behind and they
all moved so slowly, it seemed like it would take forever to get where
they were going. But it hardly mattered. There is lots of time when
you are dead. Those processions made me dread and look forward to
Sunday at the same time.

The church services were held in Korean, so a massive Sunday
school system existed to accommodate all the exclusively English-
speaking kids. It was broken down into two groups, the baby classes
with Jesus coloring books and the Methodist Youth Foundation,
which was for the teenagers who cut class and went into Chinatown
to smoke cigarettes and talk about what they'd done Saturday night.
When they did go to class, it was like a cool "rap" session, involving
young pastors getting out their acoustic guitars and talking about the
"downer" of premarital sex.

They hated me there. Everyone. From the babies all the way
to the teenagers. Maybe the teachers and the young pastor didn't,
because they'd spend time trying to protect me and involve me in

some activities, the same ones the other kids would try to exclude me from. I don't think anyone could have been more hated. School was bad enough, but now it seemed like the whole world was a hostile place.

This was the '80s and I was twelve, a preteen with a Dorothy Hamill haircut and braces. Hated. Hated. Hated. I tried to ignore it, spending summers away with cousins who lived in magical Glendale, where I would sit by their swimming pool reading a waterlogged copy of *Seventeen*. Lori Laughlin set the beauty standard, and as I looked at her, my troubles would melt away. "Someday I will be seventeen…" But the thing that I couldn't admit to myself was that I was really wishing "Someday…I will be white."

Whenever I read those magazines and tried to plug into the teenage fantasy they were selling, I couldn't see myself at all. I studied those pictures and the TV and movies like *Little Darlings* over and over. Then in the mirror I would be confronted with the awful reality that I was not that. It was almost too much to bear.

My Koreanness, my "otherness" embarrassed me. When I had school projects that required the use of glue, a product my family had little need or money for, my mother would substitute leftover rice. My face would get all red and I would shake and stammer, "Why can't we have American glue!!. I hate you, Mommy!!!!" Then I would stamp my feet up the stairs and throw my hot face down on my canopy bed

Since I didn't really have friends who I was not related to, and the kinds that were cruelest to me were other Koreans, my entire world was an exercise in not belonging. The answer seemed to lie in being white, so in my fantasy life, I chose to be Lori Laughlin. In my mind, I got ready for dances, wearing only a neat white towel wrapped under my arms, spraying myself with Love's Baby Soft, wiping a cotton ball soaked in 10-0-6 lotion over my troublesome T-zone, lining my big, big eyes with Aziza by Prince Matchabelli, putting on a long, ruffled denim skirt with a petticoat underneath and then a puff-sleeved blouse with a big ruffle forming a V on my ample but not slutty chest. Then finally, I'd let my naturally curly chestnut hair fall across my narrow shoulders, pulling it up close to my head with red oval barrettes.. The only time the fantasy would change would be if I decided to be Charlene Tilton instead of Lori Laughlin, but this occurred less frequently because I read in *Teen Beat* that Charlene took forty-five minutes to blow-dry her hair, which even then I found unreasonable.

I usually never got to the dance, because my fantasies were all about getting ready, looking a certain way, about not being me. How sad to use such a rich and vibrant imagination to dream about grooming, and not only that but grooming someone else.

Sometimes, I would get so caught up in the fantasy that I would actually go to the dance, but since I'd never been to one yet, that image was rather muddled. I'd end up slow-dancing to Air Supply with the cutest guy in my grade, Steve Goldberg, a hot Jewish kid with blonde hair and a huge ass. Steve was relentlessly mean to me, perhaps because he knew I had a crush on him, but he was also in his own pain because of his big behind. Once, an a field trip he made all the kids in the class say "Hi Margaret" to a big golden retriever as they walked by "Hey everybody, say hi to Margaret. She's a dog! Get it!" I wasn't offended. I always thought dogs were beautiful. It hurt me only because it was meant to, but it was nothing compared to the treatment I got at church.

It started with my name. I was born Moran Cho. Moran is a Korean name, meaning peony flower, a plant that blooms even in the harshest winter. My father gave me this thoughtful, unusual name without the knowledge that someday the kids I grew up with would use it against me. It started when I was around twelve, not at school, but at church.

"MORAN!! YOU ARE NOTHIN' BUT A MORON!!!" They said my name every chance they got.

"Excuse me, but MORON didn't pass the basket this way."

"Hey! I have my hand up. You can't see me past MORON'S fat head."

"May I be moved? I don't want to sit next to MORON!"

"Jesus loves everyone, even MORON."

It was stupid, but it hurt my feelings so much. Especially since the main perpetrators had once been close friends of mine.

Lotte and Connie Park were the daughters of my parents' best friends. During the previous summer vacation, I had spent many days at their house in San Bruno. We listened to Michael Jackson's *Off the Wall*. We went down the hill to Kmart and I bought my first pair of designer jeans. We watched *Creature Features* until we were too scared and had to change the channel to *Saturday Night Live*, where we'd laugh our asses off at Steve Martin doing *King Tut*.

They told me their parents fought all night long, but when they prayed to God to make them stop, it got quiet. They said they were afraid their parents were going to get a divorce. I was scared that was going to happen to me, too. We were kids of the '80s, when divorce and nuclear war loomed large. We were afraid of being abandoned by our parents, yet excited at the possibility of peace in our homes and spending our weekends with dads we never saw as long as our parents stayed together. We also had nightmares of radioactive fallout and hoped that we'd get stuck in a bomb shelter with a cute guy.

Connie had a tendency to have sties, which gave her eyes the bubbly look of a pop-eyed goldfish, but she was thin and confident, which made her condition seem oddly attractive. Lottte looked like a Korean Genie Francis, which was exciting as this was the time when *General Hospital* ruled the airwaves—there was even a song about it, parodying the plotlines and the scandalous characters, and we'd call up KFRC and request it over and over again.

We'd commiserate about our piano teachers, the strange, old white people who would come into our homes and sit next to us as we hammered out "Close to You" on the keys. Those lessons were the one luxury my family could afford, and my brother and I suffered through them for years. Lotte and Connie would make me howl with laughter at the tales of their teacher, who would use the bathroom for up to half and hour, and help herself to Sanka in the kitchen. "Best cup I ever made…"

I don't know why it was so funny. Maybe because this was the first time anybody seemed to understand me. These girls made me feel so much less alone in the world, which made their betrayal particularly painful.

Lotte and Connie had a cousin, a shy, awkward girl named Ronny, who started going to our church. She had two older brothers who were really good-looking, with flossy, black feathered hair and tan, hard bodies, which made her popular by proxy. I was friendly to her at first, not knowing that she was to be my replacement.

One day Lotte came up to Ronny and me as we chit-chatted in the church parking lot. She looked at Ronny with a knowing glance and said, "Oh, I see you've met MORON!!!" They both started laughing hysterically and I tried to be a good sport, accepting it as some healthy ribbing among friends, even though my face got red and a knot grew in my throat. The two girls walked off and joined Connie, who was nursing a sty the size of a golf ball. They didn't speak to me again for the rest of the day, which was suspicious, but I tried to ignore it.

I went home and looked in the mirror to see if there was something wrong with me. My hair was too short; my mother had cut it into "Sheena Easton," and the feathered sides wilted in the midday heat. Maybe I was paranoid. I hoped the situation would right itself before I went off to the church summer retreat, three days in the redwoods with all the kids from MYF, a chance to be away from parents, smoke cigarettes, and bond with one another. It was Little Darlings—and although the thought of losing my virginity was a rather lofty notion for me then, at twelve, it was still in the heady mix of possibilities of being *away at camp*.

I could barely sleep the night before because I was so excited and worried at the same time. I tossed and turned and woke suddenly with the sun shining in my face, not having been aware that I had fallen asleep.

My mother drove me to the church and then inexplicably burst into tears, begging me not to go. I couldn't understand this at all. We had not been getting along lately. None of my family had. My mother and I would fight because I wouldn't practice the piano, my brother and I would fight over the TV, and my father and mother would fight all night long. I pulled away from her as she gained control of her emotions. She was cold again as I left the big yellow station wagon. I was relieved to be getting away from the fighting.

I'd hoped to get a ride with Lotte and Connie, but they'd already gone with Ronny. I was too afraid to ask Carl, the cute monkey-faced popular boy who lived to make me miserable, or Jaclyn and Eugene, the equally simian brother and sister who fancied themselves trend-setters because they'd started hating me long before anyone else.

All the kids had organized themselves into groups riding up together, and since I was late, and hated, I just stood there with my cowboy sleeping bag and tried not to look scared. I reasoned with myself that the more I worried about something bad taking place, the less likely it was to happen. Since I'd been so tortured about this trip, by this law it was bound to turn out fine.

I rode to the camp with the young minister who led the youth group. He never wore a clerical collar and was of indeterminate age—youngish, unmarried, but ageless in the way Korean men sometimes are. As his yellow Pinto puttered up the freeway, I must have fallen asleep because later, close to the camp, I woke up all sweaty.

"You are very cute when you are sleeping," Reverend Soo was always nice to me, in an uncreepy, comforting way. We got to the campsite around the middle of the day. It was hot and teeming with Korean kids. Ronny's fine-ass brother had the door of his Trans Am open, and the stereo was blasting

Chicago.

Everybody needs a little time away, just for the day…
From each other…"

The beautiful Jolie, who was a few grades above me, perfect in her cut-off jeans and ribbed purple tank, a red bandanna tied suggestively like a garter around her lean thigh, looked over at us and smiled. My heart beat faster. Jolie had never been mean to me, but she'd never spoken to me either. She was way too sophisticated for that. I had a crush on her, but I was too much in awe to even admit it to myself. Whatever Carl or Eugene did to me, it didn't matter unless *she* saw it. If *she* was a witness, then the sting of humiliation would last for days. I think it was less that I wanted her, and more that I wanted to be her. With her taut brown body and baby face, she represented to me the glory of the '80s, the idea that beauty was a powerful thing, that if you looked a certain way, you could have everything.

Around 1985, Jolie turned preppy, and her beauty, her gleam, her youthful sensuality was lost in the translation. But back then, still in her slutty prime, she held all the boys at our church in the palm of her purple-nail-polished hand.

She leaned over to Ronny's brother and whispered something. He grabbed her face and they fell into each other laughing. Oh, to laugh like that, to be held by a boy and get lost in your own wondrous being. To be able to throw your head back like a pony while the boys admired you. To be the object of desire and the one doing the desiring…I wished that for myself. As I was lost in this reverie, someone threw a pine cone at my face.

"Oh shit. MORON'S here!!!!"

I tried not to cry as I looked for the perpetrator in the crowd of kids. Jolie stifled a chuckle, biting her tantalizingly glossed lip, and turned her head away. Unable to look at me because it was just too embarrassing, she nuzzled Ronny's brother's golden neck.

The shards of pine cone made my eye blaze red. Half blind, I made it to the girl's cabin without further incident.

The cabins were made of logs. Inside, there were about ten bunk beds, which were exotic and exciting to me, as I'd never slept in one. I looked around for an unclaimed top bunk, but none was to be found. I unrolled my stained old sleeping bag that didn't zip up all the way onto the bottom bunk near the back door.

Jaclyn was in the bathroom complaining to no one in particular, "The food here is so baaaddd!!! I was sticking my finger down my throat trying to throw up. That didn't work so I was on the toilet trying to *crap* it out. I want to go home!"

I wanted to go home, too. This was going to be bad. I could just tell.

Lotte came into the empty cabin and saw me. I was glad to see her and walked up.

"Hi, I just got here. Where is your bunk? I want to be near you guys," I said.

She had a mean smile on her face, but she wouldn't look me in the eye—kind of an "I can't wait to tell my friends this…" expression.

She said, "We're over there. It's too crowded already. I'm going to the canoes."

"Well, wait for me. I'm going to change and come down too.."

I ran over to my bunk to get my bathing suit, but she was already gone.

I put on my orange one-piece and an oversize white T-shirt and walked down to the lake.

Carl saw me first.

"Oh shit. It's Moron. Let's drown her. Hey Moron. Why'd you come here? Nobody likes you. It's going to be the worst three days of your life."

"Shut up!" I yelled.

Carl's brother Mike jumped in.

"Don't tell my brother to shut up! You shut up, Moron! MORON!!!!"

I tried to ignore them and got into a boat by myself. Not really knowing how to row, I pushed back from the dock a few feet and panicked. I must have only been about five feet away, but it might as well have been miles because I couldn't move the boat back at all. I was slowly drifting out onto the lake. I envisioned myself washed ashore on a deserted island, far away from the taunts and flying pine cones, meeting Christopher Atkins there in our own *Blue Lagoon*, eating bananas and wearing a loincloth and having sex for the very first time…

Carl and Mike started to miss me, I guess, because they started to scream at me.

"MORON! MORON! Just paddle it back. Don't hog the boat, pig! Boat Hog! MORON!!!!"

Lotte, Connie, and Ronnie joined them on the dock. They all started yelling. "MORON!!! God! Can't you do anything?

Just paddle it back. We want to go, too, MORON!!! Stupid.
C'mon. Hurry!"

I was trying to make the oars move in the water, but they
were too heavy. The boat started to drift back toward the dock,
but not nearly as quickly as they would have liked, so they
all screamed louder.

"MORON! Can't do anything! Why don't you just go home!
You're ruining it for everybody. MORON! WE hate YOU!!!
MORON!!! GO HOME! GO HOME! GO HOME! GO HOME!!!!"

A camp counselor, one of the older Korean girls in Jolie's class,
came down to the dock. "Just row it. Just hold the oar. No! Just—
come on! Other people want to use the boat, too. Come on. Don't
be so selfish. Just row back here. Come on!"

"Yeah, MORON. Do what she says. Come on, MORON!
MORON MORON MORON MORON MORON!!!!!!!!"

I was not going to cry. I was too old for that. I was not going
to give them the satisfaction. My face was red, and my eye still
burned from the pine cone. My arms were killing me from rowing.
Finally, with a pull on the oars that took all of my strength, the boat
banged on the dock.

Carl jumped in the boat and tried to push me in the water, but I
was fast and ran back to the girls' cabin.

The cabin was quiet. Everybody was off doing something
fun, enjoying the time away from home with friends, getting tan,
doing arts and crafts, playing volleyball, going to second base in the
bushes. It made the silence unbearable.

I thought I would sleep for a while to make the time go faster. I
just wanted to go home. Why did I come? What had I been thinking?
That suddenly, when we were all away from home, I would be
friends with everyone? But then, it had been only a few weeks ago
that I was at Lotte and Connie's house, making plans about coming
to the church camp, picking out boys we liked, wishing Connie's
sty would go away before the big weekend. Was I losing my mind?
What could I have done? Carl and Mike and Jaclyn and Eugene
always hated me, but how could they so quickly infect everyone
else with that feeling? Hate was contagious, I guess. I was coming

down with it, too. I hated myself and sat down on my cowboy sleeping bag.

It made a crunching sound. I looked inside the bag. It was filled with dry leaves, pine cones, sticks and dirt---even dog shit! I heard laughter coming from outside the cabin. I recognized it. It was Lotte and Connie. I couldn't take it anymore and I started to cry. I was a million miles from home, everybody wanted me to leave, and I had just gotten here. Filling up my stained old sleeping bag was so mean, and obviously just the beginning. What else would I have to endure for the next three days?

I went outside to shake out the bag. The girls were gone. I emptied it as well as I could, but it still smelled of eucalyptus and shit. I wanted to wash it, but figured it would be even worse wet. I took it back inside and sat with my head down on the bottom bunk.

Another girl and a boy came into the cabin. A waiflike girl named May Cha stood there with her brother Johnno, a fat kid who had allergies. The area from the bottom of Johnno's nose to the top of his lip was always red and flaking off. He also had dandruff, so when he moved, it was like he was snowing.

May spoke first. "Moron, we don't want you in our cabin. You have to move. We took a vote and everybody voted to have you out."

"Where am I supposed to go?"

"I don't know. Maybe you should go and find a big tree and sleep under it. I don't care. You just can't sleep here."

"Did you fill up my sleeping bags with leaves?"

"No, I didn't do that. I just organized the vote to have you kicked out of the cabin. I wouldn't do something like that."

I tried to think of the worst thing I could say. I knew that May wasn't responsible for the bag, but she was a dick all the same. I searched my pre-teen mind for possibilities. "Go climb a rock!" no, too Yosemite. "Sit on it." No, too *Happy Days*. Um, um. Ah, yes! I have it.

"YOUR MOTHER!!!!"

"My what?"

"YOUR MOTHER!!!!"

Johnno, who had been silent until then, exploded.

"Take that back, you bitch. What about my mother?!"

In my distress, I had forgotten that they were brother and sister, and in saying something about her mother, I was implicating him as well.

The force of his rage was truly terrifying. He got all flaky on me. It was like an avalanche. His thick glasses steamed up so fast I was sure he couldn't see me at all. It seemed somebody had said "Your mother" to him before, and he just wasn't going to take it anymore.

Johnno lunged at me and grabbed my forearms. I grabbed his in return, and we pushed each other from one side of the cabin to the other. He wasn't very strong, but he was plugged into the same kind of adrenaline that mothers use to lift cars when their children are in peril. I was so surprised that I was fighting a boy that I had trouble getting my footing. He pushed me backward into my still crunchy, cracklin'-leaves sleeping bag, and I dug my nails into his arms and pushed him up against the log wall. It must have looked like we were dancing.

Johnno's nose was running and he was crying hot, angry tears out the sides of his thick glasses. It moistened all the white patches on his upper lip so it looked like he was melting. We were getting tired of pushing each other back and forth.

He let go of my arms, and I let go of his.

"Just get out of here, MORON!"

"Yeah, get out! Get out, MORON!"

"You MORON!!! We don't want you here infecting our cabin. GET OUT GET OUT GET OUT GET OUT!!!!"

Then, inexplicably, they both left.

I took my sleeping bag to the back of the cabin and shook it out again. Leaves and twigs and dry dog turds and acorns still stuck to the flannel inside and had to be picked out by hand. I would be finding burrs embedded in my skin for days.

As I emptied the bag, I could hear the sounds of summer off in the distance. That Chicago song again, girls screaming, water splashing, intermittent outbursts of the 2-4-6-8 variety—all of it for me was the music of exclusion, the sorry soundtrack of the outcast, reminding me of all the things I was not doing, was not allowed to do, would never be a part of.

The next few days were relatively uneventful. It seems likely a talk was given, the counselors or ministers devising some intervention on my behalf. The name-calling and the shouting and the flying pine cones ceased. All that remained was a sort of silence, a wide berth. Everywhere I went for the next three days, a great deal of space was made around me. It was as if I had an infectious disease. No one would share a table or a bench with me. Not at mealtimes, not at campfires, not at the talent show that I was not allowed to participate in. In the crowded lodge, with kids crammed into every nook and cranny all over the floor, practically hanging from the rafters, I sat with an entire bench to myself. I stayed in the girl's cabin, but all the campers around me had moved their things and were sleeping on exercise mats and chairs pushed together to avoid the five bunks that surrounded mine. I got a top bunk, which I was happy about, but slept with one eye open for three days, fearing attack and ready to fight to the death.

My cootie quarantine was actually more painful than the outright battles. Everybody around me was experiencing the exhilaration of being away from home and around other kids and swinging from ropes and forging friendships that would last a lifetime, while I sat inside, alone in the shadowy cabins, and made God's Eyes out of yarn and chopsticks.

I got home, and my mother was cold and my dad was gone. She never explained where he was; she just stayed in their bedroom with the door shut.

I vowed never to return to that church, and Sunday mornings there would be a near riot with my mother begging, pleading, threatening, denying, bargaining, then finally accepting that I wasn't going with her. There was no way I was going to face those horrible kids again. I'd had enough. I was hated, so I had to hate.

My mother lied about me week after week. I think she went so far as to tell people that I was in boarding school.("She write me every day!") The abject horror at my refusal to attend church

coincided with my father's absence made her go insane. She
went on a crash diet and got down to 114 pounds and then got a
perm to celebrate.

Daddy came home eventually, like he always did, but he was
different. He was mean, cold, confusing. He kept a suitcase packed
with Gold Toe socks and underwear, ready and waiting at the bottom
of the stairs.

May Cha told my mother to tell me that she was sorry about
how they had all treated me at camp. She hoped that I would come
back someday. She said she wanted to apologize in person. I don't
know why, but that embarrassed me tremendously and made me hate
the kids even more.

I did agree to go to a church function when I was around
seventeen. I wore a flowery dress of my mother's and dyed my hair
back to black from the sick pink-orange it had been. My mother
was so happy she nearly cried and kept her arm around me the entire
time, partly out of love but also to keep me from running away.
Lotte and Connie were there, and when they saw me, their faces got
red with joy, and I wanted to punch in their hot smiles from the side.

Lotte said, "Oh, my God. MORON'S here!" I sat by my
parents, seething inside. Went home later. Never let it go.

I went on with the rest of my life. I made some good friends in
high school, and it constantly surprised me that I was never betrayed
in the same way again. Yet I didn't let myself get as close to my
friends as I would have liked.

My experience with Lotte and Connie taught me to keep people
at a distance, and not to worry about what they thought of me. In
a sense, it gave me some of the impetus I needed to go out into the
world and follow my dreams. It seemed like the worst was over. I
could get on with the business of enjoying my life, living it as fully
as possible. No matter where I was, I could be happy, since I was no
longer stuck at the summer camp, sitting on a log by myself, wishing
I had a pair of cutoffs and some friends. Loneliness became familiar
and easy. I played "Chopsticks" alone on the piano, and learned to
love every solitary note.

Not too long ago, Ronny came to a show of mine at the Punchline in San Francisco. She came backstage after the show with a group of her friends. She was thrilled to see me and wanted to talk about the days when we had known each other growing up. "Hi—remember me?" I took one look at her and said, "No, I don't. I have no idea who you are." Then I walked away.

My brother remained friendly with Lotte and Connie for years afterward. It makes me feel betrayed that he is close to them, but at least it gives me an opportunity to find out how they are doing. In some way, I suppose I miss them, because I can't seem to let go of their memory. I wish our friendship could have been allowed to grow and change and carry on into adulthood. They were horrible to me, but kids are like that sometimes. I want to forgive and be loving and try to see it from their point of view. My brother says that even now they always ask how I'm doing and are genuinely happy when he tells them, "She's just fine…"

I turned my Korean name, Moran, into one of my most lasting and memorable routines. I portray my mother screaming it through a set of French doors. "MORAN!!!!" Why would you name your daughter that? It's like calling your firstborn "Asshill." Now people call it out to me at shows---"MORAN MORAN MORAN!!!"---AND IT FEELS LIKE LOVE.

The cowboy sleeping bag sits in a closet at my parents' house. After 20 years and a lifetime of use, it still smells faintly of sap.

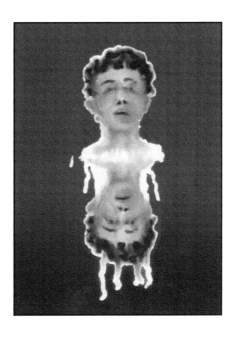

❧ *Jerry Garcia*

Becoming yourself in The Excelsior

My brother Tiff and I lived with our maternal grandparents, Bill and Tillie Clifford on Harrington Street in the Excelsior district of San Francisco. This arrangement began during the devastating emotional aftermath of my father's accidental death by drowning in 1947.

Bill Clifford and Tillie Olsen were an odd couple. I mean really odd. As a kid, of course, I found no contradiction in their relationship (I didn't notice any). It's only with the so-called sophistication of adulthood that some of the more bizarre details stand out as being the least bit unconventional. A large part of the "oddness" I referred to seemed to be an enormous mismatch of personality types…enormous differences in personality, style and energy, differences so vast that I, at any rate, am totally unable to imagine what could have attracted them to each other in the first place. They never talked about each other, much less reminisced about their courtship. In fact, I don't really remember them talking to each other at all.

She was a handsome woman, and probably had been a beautiful girl, at least that was what my brother and I believed when we were kids.

Our bedroom boasted a large, nicely framed antique sepia portrait of a lovely woman with long black hair piled up on her head Gibson Girl style, and smoldering dark eyes. We were convinced this beauty was in fact, Tillie, our grandmother/aka Nana or "Nan" for short, when she was a girl.

She was a politician and I suppose a radical union organizer in the 30s of San Francisco laundries. She was the secretary-treasurer of the Laundry Workers Union local, A.F. of L. for as long as I can remember. This was an elected post, so Tillie would run for office down at the union hall (16th near Mission) every so often and unfailingly won in a walk—usually by an enormous margin. I actually counted ballots once, fabulously dull! She always won. I think she mostly ran unopposed. She was tremendously popular, well loved, with the rank and file (It as reciprocal, tit for tat, and she loved her members.)

Going anywhere with Nan/Tillie was always an ordeal—she always ran into friends, constituents, members of the parent union, A. F. of L. "my members" or "my girls" and bullshit with them for what seemed like weeks. I would be beside myself with exasperation, seething with impatience.

"Naaaannnn!!!" I'd yell, then, with a sigh of surrender, I'd try to amuse myself, usually by "fogging" the full-length mirror by exhaling bubble-gum flavored hot breath onto it from a distance of about one inch, or kicking those sand-filled ashtrays in what I hoped was an irritating manner, to signal (I suppose) my disapproval of these interminable hang-up schmoozings.

Every morning while my brother and I were stalling to avoid going to school until the last possible minute, Pop would go through his morning routine. First he'd shave with a straight razor, stropping it furiously for a minute or two, then balancing it delicately on the sink, sharp side out.

Next he'd whip up a delicious-looking lather in his shaving cup with one of those neat shaving brushes. Finally he'd glop it on his face, scrape it neatly off with his razor, rinse and apply liberal coats of Old Spice aftershave. Then, face gleaming pinkly, he'd go (stroll) into the kitchen to continue his morning ritual (ablutions "abh-loosions" yuk), make coffee, the old percolator kind. Then he'd go into the little antechamber adjoining the kitchen and heading toward my grandmother's room and the back stairs

The tiny room was the parrot's room, and he'd open the parrot's cage, insert a piece of sawed-off broomstick (we called it the "polly stick") that the parrot would eye suspiciously and maybe bite once or twice before gingerly climbing on and allowing him to place her gently on top of the cage. Then he'd give her fresh water, refill her parrot food dispenser and change the newspaper that lined her cage. Finally he'd replace her in the cage.

This routine of my grandfather's accompanied me from age five through young adulthood.

The parrot and the parrot routine virtually define "parrotness" in my life. The parrot's name was Loretta.

The story was this—immediately after the big San Francisco earthquake, with the city burning and the dust settling, my Grandma Tillie a little girl at the time, found the parrot walking down the street!

When my grandmother found her, she could say "prretty Loretta." She never learned anything else speechwise, at least no more English phrases. But she developed a perfectly wonderful vocabulary of environmental sounds, cars passing on Alemany Boulevard, faucets running, toilets flushing and her tour de force, an uncanny imitation of my grandmother's social club.

The social club was a collection of Nan's old homegirls from the 'hood who would rotate their meetings from one lady's house to another every Thursday night for an evening of cards and liquor that would get progressively more raucous as the hours passed.

The bird could do a perfectly marvelous imitation of the whole deal, cards shuffling, poker chips rattling, ice cubes clinking, old lady voices gabbing...gales of hysterical laughter.

I mean it was truly fabulous and absolutely unmistakable.

My family, being mostly Irish-Spanish, was nominally Catholic, that is, the kids go to church on Sundays and holy days like Ash Wednesday, all rites and sacraments, i.e.: christenings, baptisms, communions, confirmations, weddings and funerals were held under the auspices of Mother Church. When I lived at 87 Harrington Street, the neighborhood church was Corpus Christi (body of Christ) located one block northeast of Harrington Street and occupying about one half block of an area. It was, when we first moved there, a typical wooden frame, sort of classic little old church-in-the-lane cum here's the church, there's the people, open the door, etc....kind of deal.

It was part of a larger complex including convent, primary school, residences for priests and nuns, chapels...Like I said, about half-a-block area in all.

Anyway, in 1949 they tore the whole complex down and started building an ultramodern, no crosses, no statuary, no steeple, rectangular Bauhaus kind of nontraditional church. This transformation was occurring throughout the diocese, and strange modern churches were springing, like weird mutant mushrooms, up all over the place.

As I recall it, the parishioners at the time were not very happy with these angular, bizarre, clearly nontraditional, possibly even heretic intruders into the familiar forms and wholesome shapes that represent God's House, Mother Church, supportive nurturing, gathering the community in...

The Excelsior district of San Francisco was ethnically mostly Italian and Irish. My family was pretty much Spanish-Irish, a stricken combination of Catholicism's Weirder Interpretations. Luckily my mother's side of the family had an iconoclastic approach—probably the union stuff—to religion so we kids were given our collection money and spruced up on Sunday morning and sent to the eight o'clock Mass and of course catechism. For non-Catholics this stuff was an impenetrable bramble of bizarre dogma, perfectly calculated to incase the seven-year-old intellect in moral concrete.

I remember worrying, with all the pious sincerity I could muster, should I happen upon a fatally wounded pagan would I have the presence of mind to correctly administer a baptism before seeking medical aid so as to ensure the survival of his/her immortal soul! Whew!

So, one block, scarcely 100 yards from the door at 87 Harrington, was God's House! In those days they still had the wonderful Latin Mass with its resonant sonorities and mysterious ritual movements, the incense, the music, choir, organ, bells, candles, the muted light through the stained glass windows.

❧ *John van der Zee*

The Big War's end. And childhood's.

When I was a child, the biggest question we could ask our parents—the one most filled with hope and awe and yearning—was this:

"What will it be like when the war is over?"

It always produced the same reaction—a misty, nostalgic look, heavy with regret that one generation was deeding to the other a childhood dominated by uniforms, violence, powerful threatening enemies and mass death. Surely such sacrifice of innocence would be rewarded.

"There'll be dancing in the streets," my mother used to say. And send me puzzled, to our front window, trying to imagine the busy San Francisco artery we lived on transformed into a dance floor. Would there be couples, or a kind of conga line? Kids jitterbugging? A sour-faced neighbor doing an ecstatic soft-shoe? The words suggested a scene so foreign, a world so transformed, that it was beyond imagery. I settled instead for a kind of Gene Kelly movie come to life: smiling people, all suddenly graceful, moving in perfect tempo to some unseen universal band---the kind of behavior, acceptable on screen, that gets people committed to institutions in life.

The day, when it came, produced not dancing in the streets, but disorder: drunkenness, smashed windows, looting, random, greedy, affectionless kissing. V-J day in San Francisco combined the worst sort of New Year's Eve party with a venting of aggressions not unlike combat itself. It took peace to bring the war home.

I wasn't there to see the disarray, or miss the dancing. Instead, along with my parents, my sisters, our cousins and an extended family of displaced urban rustics, we sat on the rickety porch of a resort cabin in Mendocino County, listening to the outside world seeping in through the radio. The announcement of the dropping of the atomic bomb, a few days before, had been momentous, but incomprehensible. This was something more personal, closer to home: the end of something deplored, yet familiar, to be replaced by a state, described by elders as normal, that was unknown.

My mother, who never smoked, handed each of us a cigarette. "I want you to do something," she said solemnly, "that you'll remember the rest of your lives." And instructed us to light up. We giggled and complied, indulged kids, sashaying around in mock sophistication, eyes watering, trying to blow rings and not gag on the early, harsh taste of growing up. It worked—both ways. I've never forgotten the day. And neither I nor my sisters smoked cigarettes.

There were parties in all the cabins, and the grownups were drinking. Not getting drunk, but high. Relieved. Absolved. At dinner in the large, communal dining room, people table-hopped, sang, called back and forth, smiled, laughed out loud, grew indulgent and voluble. So this was peace.

That day was my strongest memory of the resort called Ray's— after the husband and wife who ran it. Stronger than the memory of the girl friend (no, friend: girl) who pulled me out of the swimming

hole when I'd wandered in over my head and was near to drowning;
or the hired man section-eighted out of the Army who took me out
to watch him kill chickens, laughing as I stared in horror at their
headless, bloody running; or the snakes that sunned themselves on
the bank just below the path we walked each day to go swimming.
The strongest memory, and the last.

There were other resorts like this all over Northern California
once—rustic retreats whose minimal accommodations—my father
once turned on the shower in a Ray's cabin and a toad popped out
of the spout—were part of their charm for middle-class city people
before they took to the suburbs. But for us, there was no other Ray's.

We approached it like wagon-train emigrants, scanning the
horizon for signs of the promised land, a stifling July car, running on
rationed gas and therefore overloaded with brothers, sisters, cousins,
sometimes a dog, a crammed box of rivalries with a beleaguered
father or uncle suffering three hours of songs, games, squirming and
bickering like three on the cross.

A shout of recognition was allowed, but it too was rationed: you
had to save it till you saw The Sign—a round, rusting, once-white
metal disc, posted at a fork in the road outside the town of Philo,
with a faded name above a faded arrow. We would all cut loose then,
with a release of emotion the driver no doubt shared even as its noise
was about to burst his eardrums.

A landscape full of forest magic opened around us, a barely
cleared meadow dotted with huge blackened stumps, land grudgingly
won from dense, endless ranks of redwood and spruce; a biblical
flock of grazing sheep; and, at the road's dead end, a colonnade of
oaks so huge they all but shut out the sun. Within it, darker still,
was a cluster of log-and-clapboard cabins rich with the promise
of screened, cricket-noisy rest on sagging spring beds with mushy
concave mattresses. At the center of it all was the Ray's large
white house, our dining hall, dominated by the white tower whose
submarine-dive Klaxon summoned us to meals: Ow—oooo-gah!

"They fed you like farmhands," my father, potbellied then, later
slimly, wistfully, recalled, with Mrs. Ray herself doing the cooking:
thick, creamy, unpasteurized milk, fresh blackberries picked that day

by a vine-scratched one-armed San Francisco postman, Bill Mitchell; home-baked bread and brownies, chicken, ham, a once-a-year feast for mothers freed from kitchens, at rates so low they made staying home an extravagance. And, each Saturday night, a steak barbecue with Avon Ray delivering the meat, driving miraculously up the river bed in his yellow LaSalle, tootling "Merrily we roll along" on its multi-button horn.

Each day produced exotic, pastoral wonders: the dark, hay-and-urine secrets of an old barn; icy water from a rusty pump; water dogs; hikes through the cathedral floor of Hendy Woods: a dead, decaying deer. Once, my uncle, coming upon me fishing unsuccessfully, advised me that the proper way to catch trout was to sing to them. And left me, amiable greenhorn, standing alone beside the stream, bellowing at the top of my lungs: "Hut-sut rawl-son on the rillera!" I still got skunked.

What appealed to grownups, beyond the food and the reasonable rates, was the total absence of fashion. At the swimming hole, fat women floated about unashamedly in inner tubes, bald men wore bathing caps, people lounged about in bathrobes, Panama hats, street shoes with black ankle socks. Pubescent girls wore baseball caps, ran footraces and won, swam like barracuda, neglected the soon-required, even, cosmetic tan. Fathers grew patchy cookie-duster moustaches, did belly-flops, shot pool, urban dignity checked somewhere with the starched shirts and the briefcases.

We have pictures from that summer, of my sisters, looking awkward and vulnerable, with small indication of the late-teen beauty they were to explode into; of my mother, sun-shy, sitting on the beach in a cotton dress beneath a parasol; of my father, who inexplicably thinned out as he grew older and forsook regular exercise; and myself, with steel-rimmed eyeglasses and haystack hair undeniably resembling, as people pointed out then, Froggy in the *Our Gang* comedies.

It was the best summer, and the last. By the next June, my sisters, heeding the migratory urge to go where there were "boys", led us to the Russian River, Boulder Creek, Tahoe, "better" more upscale, more glamorous places by any objective measure; But a poor substitute by mine.

I never had enough of Ray's. Much of my life since has been, I realize, an attempt to return. Yet I resisted going back to the original from simple fear that, like so much of the best of California in these years, it would be too good, too tempting to resist change. Someone would see possibilities. Develop. Improve. Incorporated it into what Tom Wolfe has aptly dubbed "the big shopping plaza of life."

So it was with wildly ambivalent feelings that, faced with absolute deadlines—my own fortieth birthday, my son's onrushing teens—I drove with my wife, son and daughter, on the day after New Year's, up the narrow Mendocino County side road that was anticipation itself of so many years before. Returning to the home I'd have liked home to be.

There was no listing in the local phone book, but the road remained, winding through land so choked with vegetation that cattle rustled about in it unseen until their heads poked out like squirrels or quail. A short way down was the sign, rusted into anonymity. Trees—bigger than I'd remembered—gave way to the hard-won meadow dotted with charred stumps—eerie monstrous figures once to us, walking this road in the dark. In the distance was the water tower, a relic the most hard-hearted developer would have kept, and below it the same large white house where the owners lived and we overate. Just beyond was the row of small cabins, *our* cabin, vacant, boarded as if condemned, yet dilapidated only in degree. The resort had aged, but not changed, and the general disrepair gave the place a curiously distinguished, autumnal survivor's glow.

We parked beside the stained white chest where bottles of pop had competed with slugs for space around the ice block. A woman came out of the house, young, kitchen-busy, wiping her hands, wearing jeans, curious at our familiarity. Mrs. Ray, she told us, long widowed, had remarried and moved to town. The young woman and her husband had bought the place several months before. She invited us into the firewood warmth of her kitchen, and introduced her husband, tall, intelligent and recently moved from Marin: people with suburban options, who had chosen to settle here. We exchanged information, names, dates, anecdotes, filling in each other's history: their Ray's for ours. The deed they bought, they told us, had been in the Ray family since the original homestead, and was signed by President Grover Cleveland. They intended to restore the place, a cabin at a time, would be taking limited guests, might allow people to pay part of their way by work, were looking to contact the old families. Ray's and its ideal owners, it seemed, had found each other.

They invited us to walk around, down the shady street, crackling with dry oak leaves; up the gaptoothed steps of our old cabin, into the slightly listing porch with the meadow sloping away to another row of cabins below, the Navarro River beyond, and the smoky blue-green forests of the Coast Range. I saw my son and daughter standing where I had stood when the war's end answered the first big question of my life. Where my mother made us remember the day, and herself.

We walked through the meadow, down the path by the second row of cabins, along the snake-bank to the swimming hole. The river ran sparkling over the rocks, without a pier or dam or a beer can in sight. There was the rock I once floundered to completely by accident—and was rewarded with a milkshake for having swum to it; the jungle-growth cove, where the water was deep enough to dive, the places where I'd caught salamanders, fished, and sang.

Bleary with nostalgia, I was not sure what my wife and children thought of this: being dragged through a decaying collection of what could pass for squatters' shacks. Yet there had been signs. My son had pried an opening in one of our old cabin's barricading boards, his curiosity to go inside greater than my own. My daughter asked question after question about what we did here, as children, my sisters and I; my wife had her own rare light of recognition in her eye.

Standing in the vandalized social hall, half-charred, floorboards missing but with an inviting fieldstone fireplace and fan-backed lattice chairs, my daughter said: "Dad, when can we come and stay here?"

The life that Ray's and resorts like it represented—modest family joys, indulgence within limits, an inward-looking husbandry of summer freedoms—has all but disappeared from the California of these years, obscured by clouds of speed boat spray and camper dust. Yet it's restorable, through work and love, like a woody station wagon forgotten in a barn. It's about time for people to rediscover the pleasures of going to a place you don't send postcards from, and the joys of going away and staying home at the same time. It's a good life to bring back, if indeed it ever fully left us.

"There is no present or future," Eugene O'Neill, that most family-ridden of writers, once wrote. "Only the past, happening over and over again—now."

"The Last Resort" by John van der Zee from *California Livintg Magazine, the San Francisco Sunday Examiner & Chronicle*, April 4, 1976.

❧ *Author Bios*

Ansel Adams endures as one of America's most influential photographers. "Few American photographers have reached a wider audience. And none has had more impact on how Americans grasp the majesty of their continent." –from the American Experience documentary, *Ansel Adams: a Documentary Film.*

Robert Frost, is renowned for his realistic descriptions of rural life and his command of American colloquial speech. He was the recipient of four Pulitzer Prizes for Poetry. The quintessential New England poet, Frost was born in San Francisco, named after Robert E. Lee, and died in Florida.

Mae Ngai is a professor of history at Columbia University. Her Impossible Subjects won the AHA Litteton-Griswold Prize and the OAH Frederick Jackson Turner Award for best first book on any topic in American History.

Gertrude Atherton wrote for the *San Francisco Examiner*, where she met and was mentored by Ambrose Bierce. She was the author of sixty books, and dozens of articles and short stories. Her novels feature strong, independence-seeking women, and are often thought a reaction against her own marriage.

TAD, Thomas Aloysius Dorgan, was a nationally syndicated cartoonist, the most respected authority on boxing of his time, and originator of some of the most enduring and familiar expressions in American slang.

Carl Nolte, long-time reporter for the *San Francisco Chronicle*, author, historian, writer of the *Chronicle's* weekly Native Son column, is the most valued source for what is good and bad about his home town.

Frank Norris. An outstanding realist novelist of the Progressive era, Norris has been called the American Zola for his unsparing depictions of late 19th and early 20th century American life.

Isadora Duncan revolutionized dance in the 20th Century. "She alone and unhelped changed the direction of her entire art." – Agnes deMille.

James J. Corbett—"Gentleman Jim", has been called the Father of Modern Boxing because of his revolutions in training and technique. In 1892, he knocked out the famous John L. Sullivan for the world's Heavyweight Championship.

Anita Loos was the writer of more than two hundred film scenarios and screenplays, including the screenplay for the film *San Francisco*. Her novel *Gentlemen Prefer Blondes* ran through 85 editions and translations into 14 languages, including Chinese.

Robert McNamara was president of Ford Motor Company, Secretary of Defense under John F. Kennedy, Secretary of State under Lyndon Johnson, then president of the World Bank. He helped lead the nation into the Vietnam War, and spent the rest of his life pondering its moral consequences.

Robert Carson is a published poet, a produced lyricist, a screenwriter whose work has been directed by Bertrand Tavernier, and, for more than three decades, a member of the International Longshoremen's and Warehousemen's Union.

Carol Channing originated on Broadway the musical-comedy roles of Lorelei Lee in *Gentlemen Prefer Blondes* and Dolly Gallagher Levi in *Hello Dolly*. She is the recipient of three Tony Awards, including one for lifetime achievement, a Golden Globe and an Oscar nomination.

Joe DiMaggio, a member of the Baseball Hall of Fame, was a three-time winner of baseball's Most Valuable Player award, a 13-time All-Star (the only player selected for the All-Star game in every year he played). His 56-game hitting streak is a record that has lasted for more than 70 years.

Kevin J. Mullen is remembered as an historian, author, and longtime member of the San Francisco Police Department, from which he retired as Deputy Chief.

Maya Angelou's autobiography, *I Know Why The Caged Bird Sings*, brought her an international reputation and was nominated for a National Book Award. She has been awarded over 30 honorary degrees and was nominated for a Pulitzer Prize for poetry in 1971.

Rube Goldberg was a cartoonist, sculptor, author, engineer and inventor. He is best known for a series of popular cartoons depicting complex devices that perform simple tasks in indirect, convoluted ways—now known as Rube Goldberg machines, a term that has entered the dictionary.

Ernest Lageson was a practicing attorney for more than 45 years, and an internationally known trial lawyer. He is the author of several books, most notably *Battle of Alcatraz*, a nonfiction account of the 1946 escape attempt, the most famous in the island's history.

John Patrick Diggins is generally regarded as the leading intellectual historian of his generation.. The author of sixteen books, including the National Book Award finalist *Mussolini and Fascism: The View from America*, he was a Distinguished Professor at the Graduate Center of the City University of New York.

Gus Lee attended the U.S. Military Academy at West Point, did graduate work in East Asian History and obtained a law degree from the University of California at Davis where he served as Assistant Dean of Students. He later served as a U.S. Army Command Judge Advocate and a U.S. Senate ethics investigator. His memoir/ novel *China Boy* became San Francisco's first One City One Read selection.

Anne Lamott is a novelist, memoirist and speaker cherished for her transparency and humor. The author of six novels and three autobiographical books, her *Bird by Bird* is perhaps the most sympathetic book ever written about the craft and cross of writing.

Sean Wilsey is the best-selling author of *Oh The Glory of It All*, and co-editor of *State by State: A Panoramic Portrait of America*. He currently lives in New York, where he is editor at large for *McSweeney's Quarterly Concern*.

Lincoln Mitchell is an Associate at Columbia University's Harriman Institute. From 2006-2009 he was the Arnold A. Saltzman Assistant Professor at Columbia. Before joining Columbia's faculty, he was a practitioner of political development and continues to work in that field.

Margaret Cho is a comedian, fashion designer, actress, author and recording artist, best-known for her standup comedy through which she critiques social and political problems, especially those relating to race and sexuality. She has won awards for her work in behalf of women, Asians, and the gay, lesbian, bisexual and transgender community.

Jerry Garcia was a prolific musician, composer, and singer, one of the founders of (and unofficial spokesman for) The Grateful Dead. He also released several solo albums and contributed to the work of other artists as a session musician. He was known by many for his distinctive guitar work, and was ranked by **Rolling Stone** as 13th among the 100 greatest guitarists of all time.

John van der Zee is the author of a dozen books, including the bestseller *The Gate: The True Story of the Design and Construction of The Golden Gate Bridge*. His work has appeared in *The New York Times, The San Francisco Chronicle, the San Francisco Examiner, The Los Angeles Times, Town & Country* and *salon.com*